Real

Writing 1

with answers

Graham Palmer

CAMBRIDGE
UNIVERSITY PRESS

CAMBRIDGE UNIVERSITY PRESS

Cambridge, New York, Melbourne, Madrid, Cape Town, Singapore, São Paulo, Delhi

Cambridge University Press
The Edinburgh Building, Cambridge CB2 8RU, UK

www.cambridge.org
Information on this title: www.cambridge.org/9780521701846

First published 2008

Printed in the United Kingdom at the University Press, Cambridge

A catalogue record for this publication is available from the British Library

ISBN-13 978-0-521-70184-6

Contents

Map of the book

Work and Study

Acknowledgements

This book is dedicated to Wendy Gunn. The author would like to thank Nóirín Burke, Martine Walsh, Roslyn Henderson, Caroline Thiriau and Laila Friese for their vision, patience and tireless work; and Karen, James and Isobel for hugs and understanding.

The author and publishers are grateful to the following reviewers for their valuable insights and suggestions:

Kathryn Alevizos, UK
Vanessa Boutefeu, Portugal
Helen Cocking, UK
Stephanie Dimond-Bayir, UK
Philip Dover, UK
Rosie Ganne, UK
Peter Gray, Japan
Jean Greenwood, UK
Sharon Hartle, Italy
Duncan Hindmarch, UK
Rania Khalil Jabr, Egypt
Hanna Kijowska, Poland
Philip Lodge, Dubai
Marc Sheffner, Japan
Wayne Trotman, Turkey
Tadeusz Z. Wolansk, Poland

The authors and publishers acknowledge the following sources of copyright material and are grateful for the permissions granted. While every effort has been made, it has not always been possible to identify the sources of all the material used, or to trace all copyright holders. If any omissions are brought to our notice, we will be happy to include the appropriate acknowledgements on reprinting.

p. 13: the MASTERCARD trademark with permission of MasterCard International; pp. 14, 15, 17: Royal Mail 'signed for', 'customs' and 'registered' forms, © Royal Mail Group Ltd 2007; p. 17: the Post Canada 'registered' form, © 2007 Canada Post Corporation; pp. 19–21: the NatWest credit card application form with permission of the Royal Bank of Scotland Group.

The publishers are grateful to the following for permission to reproduce copyright photographs and material:

Key: l = left, c = centre, r = right, t = top, b = bottom

Alamy Images/©D Hurst for p. 18 (b)/©Nigel Sawtell for p. 34 (l)/©Simon Reddy for p. 47; Corbis Images/©Mike Watson Images for p. 18 (t)/©Free Agents Ltd for p. 38 (cl)/©Guenter Rossenbach/Zefa for p. 38 (br)/©Royalty Free for p. 81; Getty Images/Stone for p. 30 (tr)/©Stone for p. 30 (bl)/©AFP for p. 38 (t)/©National Geographic for p. 38 (cr)/©Robert Harding for p. 38 (bl); Photolibrary.com/©Imagestate Ltd for p. 10 (b); Punchstock/©Inspirestock for p. 10 (t)/©Stockbyte for p. 30 (tl)/©Image Source for p. 30 (br)/©Stockbyte for p. 49 (l)/©Comstock for p. 49 (r); Rex for p. 34 (r)/p. 42; Staples.co.uk for p. 79; Superstock/©Age fotostock for pp. 46 and 62.

Front cover of *Why Does a Ball Bounce* by Adam Hart-Davis on p. 58, Ebury Press, 2005. Reprinted by permissions of The Random House Group Ltd.

Front cover in its entirety of *The Hound of the Baskervilles* by Arthur Conan Doyle and editied by Christopher Frayling on p. 60 (Penguin Books 2001)

Front cover of *The Crocodile Hunter* by Steve & Terri Unwin on p. 78 (r), Orion Books, a division of The Orion Publishing Group

Front cover of *Things Fall Apart* by Chinua Achebe on p. 78 (l), Penguin Books, 2006

Illustrations:

Kathy Baxendale pp. 10b, 30t, 54b; Mark Duffin pp. 13, 16, 28, 29, 30b, 31, 33b, 42b, 44, 45, 54t, 56, 60, 65, 70, 71, 76; Kamae Design pp. 35; Katie Mac pp. 22, 24, 32, 33t, 72; Laura Martinez pp. 26, 42t, 63; Julian Mosedale pp. 37, 40, 50, 66; Valeryia Steadman pp. 12, 14, 27, 58, 74; Mark Watkinson pp. 10t, 15; Ian West pp. 47, 64

Text design and page make-up: Kamae Design, Oxford
Cover design: Kamae Design, Oxford
Cover photo: © Getty
Picture research: Hilary Luckcock

Introduction

To the student

Who is *Real Writing 1* for?

You can use this book if you are a student at elementary level and you want to improve your English writing. You can use the book alone without a teacher or you can use it in a classroom with a teacher.

How will *Real Writing 1* help me with my writing?

Real Writing 1 contains everyday writing practice, for example writing emails and letters and filling in forms. It is designed to help you with writing you will need to do when visiting or living in an English-speaking country.

The exercises in each unit help you develop useful skills such as planning, thinking about the reader and checking your work. It is designed to help you with writing you will need to do when communicating in English at home or when visiting another country.

How is *Real Writing 1* organised?

The book has 16 units and is divided into two sections:
- Units 1–9 – social and travel situations
- Units 10–16 – work and study situations

Every unit has:
- *Get ready to write*: to introduce you to the topic of the unit
- *Learning tip:* to help you improve your learning
- *Extra practice:* an extra exercise for more practice
- *Can-do checklist:* to help you think about what you learnt in the unit

Most units also have:
- *Did you know?*: extra information about vocabulary, different cultures or the topic of the unit
- *Focus on*: to help you study useful grammar or vocabulary
- *Class bonus:* an exercise you can do with other students or friends

After each section there is a review unit. The reviews help you practise the skills you learn in each section.

At the back of the book you can find:
- *Appendices*: contain lists of *Useful language* for every unit and more ideas about how to improve your writing
- *Audioscript*: includes everything that you can hear on the audio CD and gives information about the nationalities of the speakers.
- *Answer key*: (only in the with answers edition) gives correct answers and possible answers for exercises that have more than one answer.

How can I use *Real Writing 1*?

The units at the end of the book are more difficult than the units at the beginning of the book. However, you do not need to do the units in order. It is better to choose the units that are most interesting for you and to do them in the order you prefer.

There are many different ways you can use this book. We suggest you work in this way:
- Look in the *Contents* list and find a unit that interests you.
- Go to *Appendix 1: Useful language* and look at the wordlist for the unit you want to do. You can use a dictionary to help you understand the words.
- Or look at *Appendix 2: What can I improve?* and find a unit that is useful for you.
- Do the *Get ready to write* section at the start of the unit. This will help you think about the topic of the unit.
- Do the other exercises in the unit in order. At the end of each exercise check your answers with your teacher or in the *Answer key*.
- Try to do the listening exercises without looking at the *Audioscript*. You can read the *Audioscript* after you finish the exercises.
- If your answers are wrong, study the section again to see where you made mistakes.
- After you finish the *Write* exercise use the *Check* checklist to correct your writing. You can also use *Appendix 3: Check your writing* and *Appendix 4: Check your mistakes* to check your writing.
- If you want to do more work on this topic, do the *Extra practice* activity.
- At the end of the unit, think about what you learnt and complete the *Can-do checklist.*
- Go to *Appendix 1* and look at the *Useful language* for the unit again.

Introduction
To the teacher

What is *Cambridge English Skills*?

Real Writing 1 is one of 12 books in the *Cambridge English Skills* series. The series also contains *Reading* and *Listening & Speaking* books and offers skills training to students from elementary to advanced level. All the books are available in with-answers and without-answers editions.

Level	Book	Author
Elementary CEF: A2 Cambridge ESOL: KET NQF Skills for life: Entry 2	Real Reading 1 with answers	Liz Driscoll
	Real Reading 1 without answers	Liz Driscoll
	Real Writing 1 with answers and audio CD	Graham Palmer
	Real Writing 1 without answers	Graham Palmer
	Real Listening & Speaking 1 with answers and audio CD	Miles Craven
	Real Listening & Speaking 1 without answers	Miles Craven
Pre-intermediate CEF: B1 Cambridge ESOL: PET NQF Skills for life: Entry 3	Real Reading 2 with answers	Liz Driscoll
	Real Reading 2 without answers	Liz Driscoll
	Real Writing 2 with answers and audio CD	Graham Palmer
	Real Writing 2 without answers	Graham Palmer
	Real Listening & Speaking 2 with answers and audio CD	Sally Logan & Craig Thaine
	Real Listening & Speaking 2 without answers	Sally Logan & Craig Thaine
Intermediate to upper-intermediate CEF: B2 Cambridge ESOL: FCE NQF Skills for life: Level 1	Real Reading 3 with answers	Liz Driscoll
	Real Reading 3 without answers	Liz Driscoll
	Real Writing 3 with answers and audio CD	Roger Gower
	Real Writing 3 without answers	Roger Gower
	Real Listening & Speaking 3 with answers and audio CD	Miles Craven
	Real Listening & Speaking 3 without answers	Miles Craven
Advanced CEF: C1 Cambridge ESOL: CAE NQF Skills for life: Level 2	Real Reading 4 with answers	Liz Driscoll
	Real Reading 4 without answers	Liz Driscoll
	Real Writing 4 with answers and audio CD	Simon Haines
	Real Writing 4 without answers	Simon Haines
	Real Listening & Speaking 4 with answers and audio CD	Miles Craven
	Real Listening & Speaking 4 without answers	Miles Craven

Where are the teacher's notes?

The series is accompanied by a dedicated website containing detailed teaching notes and extension ideas for every unit of every book. Please visit www.cambridge.org/englishskills to access the *Cambridge English Skills* teacher's notes.

What are the main aims of *Real Writing 1*?

- To help students develop writing skills in accordance with the ALTE (Association of Language Testers in Europe) Can-do statements. These statements describe what language users can typically do at different levels and in different contexts. Visit www.alte.org for further information.
- To encourage autonomous learning by focusing on learner training

What are the key features of *Real Writing 1*?

- It is aimed at elementary learners of English at level A2 of the Council of Europe's CEFR (Common European Framework of Reference for Languages).
- It contains 16 four-page units, divided into two sections: Social and Travel, and Work and Study.
- *Real Writing 1* units contain:
  - *Get ready to write* warm-up exercises to get students thinking about the topic
  - *Learning tips* which give students advice on how to improve their writing and their learning
  - *Focus on* exercises which provide contextualised practice, in particular language or vocabulary areas
  - *Class bonus* communication activities for pairwork and group work so you can adapt the material to suit your class
  - *Did you know?* boxes which provide notes on cultural or linguistic differences between English-speaking countries, or factual information on the topic of the unit
  - *Extra practice* exercises which give students a chance to find out more information about the topic for themselves.
  - *Can-do checklists* at the end of every unit to encourage students to think about what they have learnt.
- There are two review units to practise skills that have been introduced in the units.
- *Real Writing 1* has an international feel and contains a range of native and non-native English accents.
- It can be used as self-study material, in class or as supplementary homework material.

What is the best way to use *Real Writing 1* in the classroom?

The book is designed so that there is no set way to work through the units. The units may be used in any order, although the more difficult units naturally appear near the end of the book, in the Work and Study section.

You can consult the unit-by-unit teachers' notes at www.cambridge.org/englishskills for detailed teaching ideas. However, broadly speaking, different parts of the book can be approached in the following ways:

- *Useful language:* You can use the *Useful language* lists in the Appendices to preteach or revise the vocabulary from the unit you are working on.
- *Get ready to write:* It is a good idea to use this section as an introduction to the topic. Students can work on the exercises in pairs or groups. Many of these exercises require students to answer questions about their personal experience. These questions can be used as prompts for discussion. Some exercises contain a problem-solving element that students can work on together. Other exercises aim to clarify key vocabulary in the unit. You can present these vocabulary items directly to students.
- *Learning tips:* You can ask students to read and discuss these in an open-class situation. An alternative approach is for you to create a series of discussion questions associated with the *Learning tip*. Students can discuss their ideas in pairs or small groups followed by open-class feedback. The *Learning tip* acts as a reflective learning tool to help promote learner autonomy.
- *Class bonuses*: The material in these activities aims to provide freer practice. You can set these up carefully, then take the role of observer during the activity so that students carry out the exercise freely.
- *Extra practice:* These can be set as homework or out-of-class projects for your students. Alternatively, students can do some exercises in pairs during class time.
- *Can-do checklists:* Refer to these at the beginning of a lesson to explain to students what the lesson will cover, and again at the end so that students can evaluate their learning for themselves.
- *Appendices:* You may find it useful to refer your students to the *Check your writing* and *Check your mistakes* sections. Students can use these as general checklists to help them in their written work.

Get ready to write

Xiaoping

Think about these questions:

○ Where is Xiaoping? What is he doing?

○ Which room do you think he wants? Why?

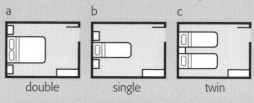

a   b   c

double   single   twin

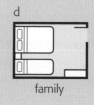

d

family

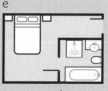

e

en suite

go to Useful language p. 82

The George Guest House

615 George Street, Sydney, New South Wales, 2000, Australia
Phone: +61 2 9355 8766 Fax: +61 2 9354 8768
Email: info@georgegh.com.au

Booking Form

Please use BLOCK CAPITALS.

1 Full name   XIAOPING WANG
2 Address   12-4A, DONG RUN FENG JING, SOUTH DONG FENG ROAD,
         CHAOYANG DISTRICT, BEIJING PRC
3 Post code   100027
4 Tel no.   +86 010 6441 3576

5 Number of guests   1
6 Type of room   single/~~double/twin/family~~ Delete as appropriate
7 Age of children   N/A
8 Date of arrival   22/3/07
9 Date of departure   23/3/07
   Method of payment   MasterCard ✓   Visa ☐   Cheque ☐   Tick
   Credit card no.   5442 8777 8990 2453
   Expiry Date   08 09
   Signature   王小平

N.B. All our rooms are en suite and cost $110 (AUS) per person. This price includes breakfast.

Completing hotel forms

Look at an example

1 **Look at the form. Find the answer to these questions. For each answer write a red number from the form.**

   a   What's your first and last name? ☐ 1
   b   How old are your children? ☐
   c   Where do you live? ☐
   d   What's your telephone number? ☐
   e   What's your post code? ☐
   f   When are you coming? ☐
   g   When are you going? ☐

2 Match the instructions with the examples.

a Please tick
b Circle
c Delete as appropriate
d Signature
e Use BLOCK CAPITALS

1 single / double / twin / family
2 single / double / twin / (family)
3 single ☐ double ☐
   twin ✓ family ☐
4 JANE BOULSON
5 J Boulson

3 Are these true (T) or false (F)?

a N.B. = This is not important information. F
b N/A = I do not need to give an answer. ......
c Date (UK / Australia) = Day / Month / Year ......

Did you know ...?

Full name = first name + last name
NOT   last name + first name
Date (UK / Australia) = Day / Month / Year
BUT
Date (US) = Month / Day / Year
Post code (UK) = Zip code (US)

4 Write these dates in numbers.

		UK	US
a	2 December 2007	2/12/07	12/2/07
b	8 April 2010		
c	13 July 2008		
d	30 September 2012		

Focus on ...
the alphabet

1 The receptionist wrote down the names of guests. She has made some mistakes.
   🔊2 Listen and underline the mistakes.

The George Guest House

a Room 1: Anna Konti
b Room 2: Jane Poulson
c Room 3: Jordon McNamara
d Room 4: Edwardo Silva

2 Listen again and correct the mistakes.
   E.g. Room 1: Anna Conti

Plan

5 Write your full name in BLOCK CAPITALS and add your signature.

Name
Signature

6 Write your post/zip code.

Post / Zip code

7 Write today's date.

Date

Learning tip

It is easy to make a mistake on a form. Use a pencil when you first fill in a form. When you finish, check your answers and then complete the form in pen.

Class bonus

1 Work with a partner.
   Student A: Look at Card 1.
   Student B: You are the receptionist. Write down the guest's name and address.

2 Student A: You are the receptionist. Write down the guest's name and address.
   Student B: Look at Card 2.

3 With your partner, check to see if the receptionist has spelt the name and address correctly.

Cards for students A and B

1 Student A: Your name is George Barras and you are English. You live at 84 Chalmers Road, Cambridge CB8 5LL, UK. You want to stay at the George Guest House. Telephone to make a reservation.

2 Student B: Your name is Mahmoud Boutaleb. You live at 51 Gezira El Wosta Street, Apartment 6, Zamalek, Cairo 1511, Egypt. You want to stay at the George Guest House. Telephone to make a reservation.

Focus on ...
CAPITAL LETTERS

1 (Circle) the capital letters
   in this sentence.
   (L)ast week, I stayed in
   your New York hotel from
   Monday to Wednesday.

2 True (T) or false (F)?
   These words always begin
   with a capital letter:
   a names of people, days,
      places, languages,
      nationalities ..T..
   b things ......
   c the first word in a
      sentence ......
   d first person personal
      pronoun, e.g.(I)am
      sixteen years old. ......

3 The guest in the picture was
   not happy with his hotel.
   Why was he unhappy?

4 The shift key on the writer's
   computer is broken. He does
   not use any capitals. Correct
   the mistakes.

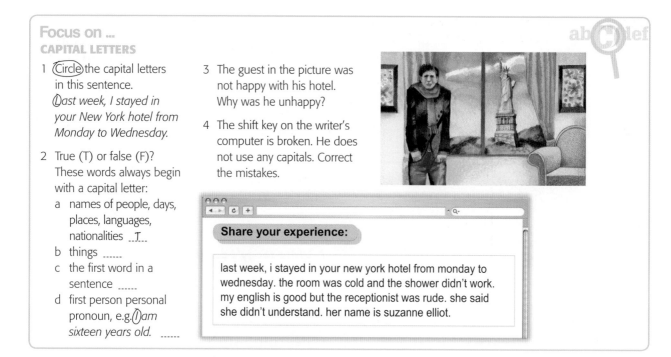

Share your experience:

last week, i stayed in your new york hotel from monday to
wednesday. the room was cold and the shower didn't work.
my english is good but the receptionist was rude. she said
she didn't understand. her name is suzanne elliot.

Write

8 **You want to visit New York with a friend. You want to stay for seven nights starting on 24 March.
   Complete this online registration form.**

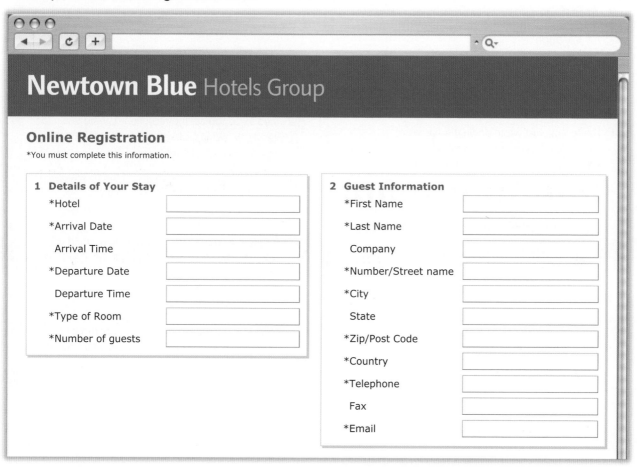

Newtown Blue Hotels Group

Online Registration
*You must complete this information.

1 Details of Your Stay

*Hotel

*Arrival Date

Arrival Time

*Departure Date

Departure Time

*Type of Room

*Number of guests

2 Guest Information

*First Name

*Last Name

Company

*Number/Street name

*City

State

*Zip/Post Code

*Country

*Telephone

Fax

*Email

9 **Use the information from this card to complete the payment information part of the form.**

---

3 Payment information

*Type of Card:	◑ Mastercard ◑ Visa ◑ Diners Club ◑ AmEx ◑ JCB
*Card number	
*Name on Card	
Expiry date	

Check

– Have you completed all the necessary information (*)?
– Have you used capital letters for your name, street name, city and country?
– Have you used the right form of date for the US (Month/Day/Year)?

E✗tra practice

– Think of a city you would like to visit. Search the Internet for the website of a hotel in that city.
– If the hotel has an online enquiry form, complete it. When the hotel replies check that they have understood your enquiry.
– If the hotel does not have an online enquiry form, print out the hotel's booking form and complete it. Use the **Check** checklist to correct the form. Ask your teacher or a native speaker to check your completed form.

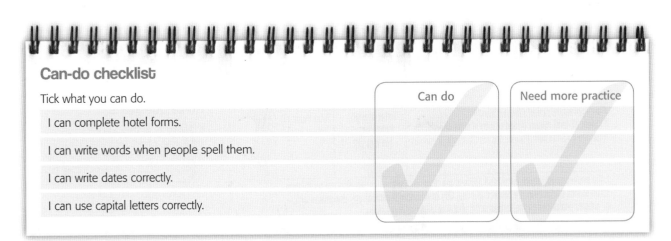

Can-do checklist

Tick what you can do.

	Can do	Need more practice
I can complete hotel forms.		
I can write words when people spell them.		
I can write dates correctly.		
I can use capital letters correctly.		

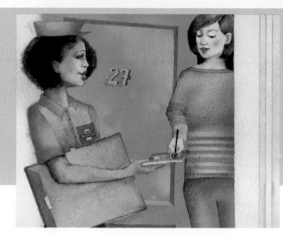

go to Useful language p. 82

Completing post office forms

Look at an example

1 Use information from forms **A** and **B** on pages 14 and 15 to complete the gaps or write 'Don't know'.

Form	Who is sending the mail?	Who is going to receive it?
A		
B	Celine Dupont	

Form A Celine is sending a birthday present to a friend in another country. She has completed a customs declaration form.

CUSTOMS DECLARATION
DÉCLARATION EN DOUANE
CN 22
May be opened officially
Peut être ouvert d'office

Great Britain\Grande-Bretagne   **Important! See instructions on the back**

✓	Gift\Cadeau		Commercial sample\Echantillon commercial
	Documents		Other\Autre *Tick one or more boxes*

Quantity and detailed description of contents (1) Quantité et description détaillée du contenu	Weight (*in kg*)(2) Poids	Value (3) Valeur
1 DVD	0.09kg	£15.00

For commercial items only If known, HS tariff number (4) and country of origin of goods (5) Nºtarifaire du SH et pays d'origine des marchandises (si connus)	Total Weight Poids total (*in kg*) (6)	Total Value (7) Valeur totale

I, the undersigned, whose name and address are given on the item, certify that the particulars given in this declaration are correct and that this item does not contain any dangerous article or articles prohibited by legislation or by postal or customs regulations

Date and sender's signature (8)   *C. Dupont   22/06/07*

2 Read form A and answer these questions.

a What is in the parcel?
   .... *a DVD* ....
b How heavy is it?
   ....
c How much did it cost?
   ....

Form B Celine wants to be sure that someone received her letter. She has completed a 'signed for' form.

Did you know …?

Mail deliveries and post office forms are different in different countries. In some countries *Signed for* mail is called *recorded* or *certified mail*.

Some other types of mail:
Registered mail: This is recorded mail for valuable items. It is tracked and insured. You can get compensation if it is lost or damaged.
Special Delivery/Express/Priority = guaranteed next day or early delivery.

---

3 Look at this part of form B.

What do you write first in an address? Put the list below into the correct order.

a post code ☐
b house number 1
c road ☐
d city ☐

4 **Look at the capital letters and commas (,) in Celine's address. Write this address correctly.**

467 queensferry road edinburgh eh9 7nd

Focus on …
weight

We write …	We say …
1.5 kg	one point five kilos/kilograms NOT 1,5 kg
0.75 kg	(UK) 'o' point seven five kilos NOT 'o' point seventy-five kilos
	(US) zero point seven five kilos

1 🔊**4** A friend asked you to take these parcels to the post office. He guessed the weight of the parcels. Listen to the man in the post office and correct any weights that are wrong.

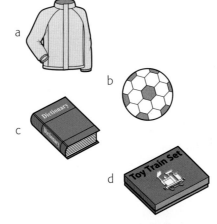

Your friend's guess	Actual weight
0.25 kg	2.5 kg
0.42 kg	
0.25 kg	
4.6 kg	

2 How heavy do you think these things are? Write what you think in the **Your guess** boxes.

	Your guess	Actual weight
a a t-shirt		
b a DVD in its box		
c a pair of men's shoes		

3 🔊**5** Listen to the man at the post office weighing the things and write the actual weights.

Focus on ...
money

We write ...	We say ...		
40c	forty cents	NOT	c40
$4.00	four dollars	NOT	4$
$400.00	four hundred dollars	NOT	$400,00

Forty thousand euros

(UK/US/Australia) = €40,000 (or €40k)

BUT (Europe) = 40.000 € (or 40 000 €)

One dollar and forty-seven cents

(UK/US/Australia) = $1.47

BUT (Europe) = $1,47

1p   one pence/one penny/one 'p' /piː/
£9.99   nine pounds ninety-nine ('p'/pence)/ nine ninety-nine

1 Write these amounts as numbers.
   a twenty-five cents ..25c...
   b five thousand pounds ....
   c two pounds fifty ....
   d thirty dollars ....
   e three hundred and fifty pounds ....

2 🔊 **16** Listen to these people telling the man at the post office the value of their parcels. He has made some mistakes. Write the correct values.
   a Value: £575   £5.75
   b Value: $2.50   ....
   c Value: $99.00   ....
   d Value: £20.00   ....

Plan

5 Find these expressions on the forms. Are the explanations true (T) or false (F)?

   a complete in full   = do not use abbreviations ..T..
   b in ink   = do not use a pencil ......
   c tick one or more boxes = do not tick two boxes ......

6 Look at the labels on the parcels.

   a Which two labels mean 'be careful with the package'?
   b What does the other label mean?
     Send by ....

7 Look at the box. You want to send important papers to another country. Tick ✓ the correct box.

Gift \Cadeau	Commercial sample\Enchantillon commercial
Documents	Other\Autre Tick one or more boxes

8 Which type of mail would you use to send the papers in Exercise 7?

   a normal airmail ☐
   b international signed for ☐

9 Someone has asked you to send them a t-shirt.

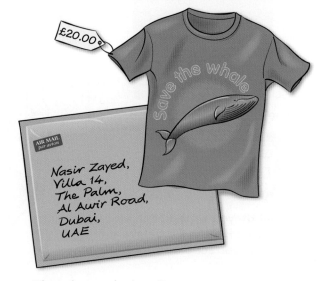

   a Who is the parcel going to?
     Nasir Zayed
     ----
   b What is his address?
     ----
   c What is in the parcel?
     ----
   d How much do you think it weighs? (Look at *Focus on weight* on page 15 to help you.)
     ----
   e How much is it worth?

Write

10 You are posting the t-shirt. Complete a customs declaration form.

Check

- Is your writing easy to read?
- Have you written what the parcel contains?
- Have you written the weight correctly?
- Have you signed your name and written today's date?

Learning tip

Words like *address* can be difficult to spell. Practise them by writing them in pairs or groups of double-letter words with similar meanings.

Examples:

1 ad<u>d</u>re<u>ss</u>, str<u>ee</u>t

2 do<u>ll</u>ar, shi<u>ll</u>ing

Look at the words. Cover them and test yourself. Try again after an hour.

CUSTOMS DECLARATION
DÉCLARATION EN DOUANE

CN 22

May be opened officially
Peut être ouvert d'office

Great Britain\Grande-Bretagne   **Important!** See instructions on the back

| | Gift\Cadeau | | Commercial sample\Echantillon commercial |
| | Documents | | Other\Autre   *Tick one or more boxes* |

Quantity and detailed description of contents (1) Quantité et description détaillée du contenu	Weight (*in kg*)(2) Poids	Value (3) Valeur
– – – – – – – – – – – –	– – –	– – –
– – – – – – – – – – – –	– – –	– – –
– – – – – – – – – – – –	– – –	– – –

For commercial items only If known, HS tariff number (4) and country of origin of goods (5) *Nºtarifaire du SH et pays d'origine des marchandises (si connus)*	Total Weight Poids total (*in kg*) (6)	Total Value (7) Valeur totale

I, the undersigned, whose name and address are given on the item, certify that the particulars given in this declaration are correct and that this item does not contain any dangerous article or articles prohibited by legislation or by postal or customs regulations

Date and sender's signature (8)

E✗tra practice

- You are travelling round Canada. You bought your Canadian friend a baseball cap for ten dollars. You want to send it to him. His name is Jon Bomberg and he lives at 153 Mountbatten Avenue, Ottawa, Ontario K1H 5V6. Complete this Post Canada form.
- Ask your teacher or a native speaker to check your form.

R	**Registered** **Domestic**	**Recommandé** **Régime intérieur**	CANADA POST / POSTES CANADA

To   Destinataire

Name   Nom

Address   Adresse

City   Ville   Province   Postal Code   Code postal

FOR DELIVERY CONFIRMATION   POUR CONFIRMER LA LIVRAISON

1 888 550-6333
www.canadapost.ca
www.postescanada.ca

Declared Value   Valeur déclarée ▶ $

Item No.   Nº de l'article
78 954 248 909

33-086-584 (98-10)

CUSTOMER RECEIPT   REÇU DU CLIENT

Can-do checklist

Tick what you can do.

	Can do	Need more practice
I can complete post office forms.	✔	✔
I can write addresses correctly.		
I can write weights correctly.		

Unit 3
At the bank

Get ready to write

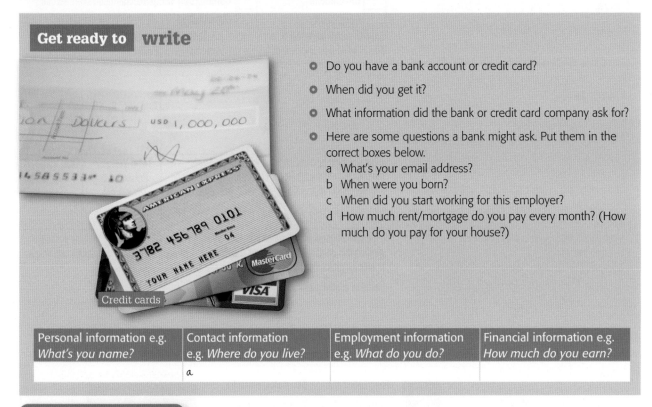

Credit cards

- Do you have a bank account or credit card?

- When did you get it?

- What information did the bank or credit card company ask for?

- Here are some questions a bank might ask. Put them in the correct boxes below.
  a What's your email address?
  b When were you born?
  c When did you start working for this employer?
  d How much rent/mortgage do you pay every month? (How much do you pay for your house?)

Personal information e.g. *What's you name?*	Contact information e.g. *Where do you live?*	Employment information e.g. *What do you do?*	Financial information e.g. *How much do you earn?*
	a		

go to Useful language p. 82

Completing bank forms

Look at an example

1 Dr Davidson wants to open a bank account. He has to complete a form. Look at this part of the form. It asks for personal details. Find the answers to the questions. Write the number(s) from the form next to the question.

a What is your name? ..2,.3..
b When were you born? ....
c Are you married? ....
d Where do you come from? ....

> ### Learning tip
>
> Before you start to complete a form, look at the headings on it. Try to guess what kind of information each section will ask for.

YOUR PERSONAL DETAILS

1 Title (*tick one*):   Mr   Mrs   Ms   Miss
   ✓ Other (*please specify*) *Dr*
2 Surname *Davidson*
3 First name(s) *John*
4 Date of birth (DD/MM/YY)   *05* / *10* / *66*
5 ✓ Male   Female
6 Single ✓ Married   Divorced/Widowed/Separated
7 Nationality *British*

2 Now write the numbers from the form that answer these questions.

a What's your home phone number? _____
b What's your email address? _____
c Where do you live? _____
d Do you own your house? _____
e Where did you live before 2006? _____

YOUR CONTACT DETAILS

8 Your telephone numbers
9 Home   0122.3 562076
10 Mobile   07812 184564
11 Work   0122.3 222323
12 Your email address   davidsonj@peacock.co.uk
13 Home address   43 Tenison Road, Cambridge
14 Post code   CB5 3FH
15 When did you start living there? (DD/MM/YY)   23 / 07 / 06
16 Residential status (tick one): ✓ Owner   Tenant   Living with relatives
17 Previous address   7 Hunar Court, Yarmouth Gardens, Shirley, Southampton
18 Postcode   BS8 2BG
19 When did you start living there? (DD/MM/YY)   17 / 03 / 01

---

3 Write the numbers from the form that answer these questions.

a What do you do? _____
b What's your employer's address? _____
c When did you start working for this university? _____

YOUR EMPLOYMENT DETAILS

20 Employment status (tick one):   Employed, full-time
21 ✓ Employed, part-time   Self-employed   Not working   Student
22   Retired   Unemployed   Other (please specify)
23 Occupation   University Lecturer
24 Employer's name   AP University
25 Employer's address   East Road, Cambridge
26 Post code   CB5 3SK
27 Date you started work with current employer (MM/YY)   09 / 05
28 Length of time with previous employer Years: 2   Months: 0

---

4 Write the numbers from the form that answer these questions.

a Have you got any savings? _____
b How much rent/mortgage do you pay every month? _____
c What's the name of the bank you use at the moment? _____

YOUR FINANCIAL DETAILS

29 Total amount of savings   £ 5,000
30 Rent/mortgage per month   £ 700.00
31 Amount to be paid into the account each month   £ 2,100
32 Do you have any other bank accounts? Yes ✓ No
33 Bank name   NatWest
34 Bank address   24 Mill Road, Cambridge
35 Post code   CB5 4FG
36 How long have you banked there? Years: 7   Months: 9
37 Your account number

Plan

5 Match the title (Mr, Miss, Mrs, Ms) to the explanation.

a Mr Peters
b Miss L Jones
c Mrs Jane Boulson
d Ms Watanabe

single woman
married woman
single or married woman
single or married man

Did you know …?

1 DD/MM/YY = Day/Month/Year.
2 Forms sometimes ask you to make a choice, e.g. Title (tick one): ☐ Mr ☐ Mrs ☐ Ms ☐ Miss
Often they include this choice: ☐ Other (please specify). _____
If the choices they give are not correct for you, write something that is correct for you, e.g. Dr
3 Forms also sometimes ask for mother's maiden name. This is the surname your mother had before she was married.

6 Complete the nationalities.

I'm from …	I'm ___ish
Britain.	a I'm British _____
Turkey.	b I'm _____
I'm from …	I'm ___ese.
China.	c I'm _____
Japan.	d I'm _____
I'm from …	I'm ___an.
Russia.	e I'm _____
Mexico.	f I'm _____
g Write your nationality	
_____	

7 Complete this puzzle. Use words from YOUR EMPLOYMENT DETAILS on page 19.

Clues

a You work 35 hours every week. You work
f _ _ _ - t _ _ _ .

b You do not work. You are u _ _ _ _ _ _ _ _ _ _ .

c You work for a company. You are e _ _ _ _ _ _ _ _ .

d You work for 15 hours every week. You work p_ _ _ -
t _ _ _ .

e The company you worked for before is your
p _ _ _ _ _ _ _ employer.

f You do not work for a company. You work for yourself.
You are s _ _ _ - _ _ _ _ _ _ _ _ _ .

g You are 65 years old and do not work. You are
r _ _ _ _ _ _ .

h The company you work for now is your
c _ _ _ _ _ _ employer.

Write

8 a You want to open a bank account. Complete this application form with your own details.

YOUR PERSONAL DETAILS

1 Title (*tick one*): ☐ Mr ☐ Mrs ☐ Ms ☐ Miss
☐ Other (*please specify*) _____

2 Surname _____

3 First name(s) _____

4 Date of birth (DD/MM/YY) __ / __ / __

5 ☐ Male ☐ Female

6 ☐ Single ☐ Married ☐ Divorced/Widowed/Separated

7 Nationality _____

b Now fill in your contact details.

YOUR CONTACT DETAILS

8 Your telephone numbers

9 Home _____

10 Mobile _____

11 Work _____

12 Your email address _____

13 Home address _____

14 Postcode _____

15 When did you start living there? (DD/MM/YY) __ / __ / __

16 Residential status (tick one): ☐ Owner ☐ Tenant ☐ Living with relatives

17 Previous address _____

18 Post code _____

19 When did you start living there? (DD/MM/YY) __ / __ / __

Focus on ... email addresses

Email addresses

We write …	We say …
@	at /æt/
.	dot /dɒt/
co	co /kəʊ/
com	com /kɒm/
davidsonj, uk	Spell out names and abbreviations for countries, e.g. *d-a-v-i-d-s-o-n-j*

1 🔘17 Listen to Dr Davidson. He is telling the bank manager his email address.
Write the email address.

----

2 The bank manager has written down some other customers' email addresses. She has made some mistakes. 🔘18 Listen and underline the mistakes.

a aprice@money.com
b okej@funnygirl.co.uk
c yoko@dottyhats.co.uk
d petapiper@pepper.com.au

3 🔘18 Listen again and write the correct email addresses.

a apryce@money.com
b ----------------------------
c ----------------------------
d ----------------------------

c **Now fill in your employment details.**

- -
YOUR EMPLOYMENT DETAILS
20 Employment status (tick one):   Employed, full-time
21   Employed, part-time   Self-employed   Not working   Student
22   Retired   Unemployed   Other (please specify)
23 Occupation
24 Employer's name
25 Employer's address
26 Post code
27 Date you started work with current employer (MM/YY)   /
28 Length of time with previous employer Years: Months:

EXtra practice

- Search the Internet for a bank or credit card website.
- Print out an application form.
- Complete the application form with information about you or Dr Davidson.
- Use the **Check** questions to correct the form.
- Ask your teacher or a native speaker to check your completed form.

d **You may want to use Dr Davidson's details to answer these questions.**

- -
YOUR FINANCIAL DETAILS
29 Total amount of savings   £
30 Rent/mortgage per month   £
31 Amount to be paid into the account each month   £
32 Do you have any other bank accounts? Yes   No
33 Bank name
34 Bank address
35 Post code
36 How long have you banked there? Years: Months:
37 Your account number

Check

- Is your writing easy to read?
- Have you answered all the questions?
- Have you ticked only one box ☐ for each question?
- Have you written the addresses correctly? i.e. *number + street + city*
- Have you written the dates correctly? i.e. DD/MM/YY
- Have you written the amounts correctly? e.g. £3,000

Can-do checklist

Tick what you can do.

	Can do	Need more practice
I can complete bank forms.	✓	✓
I can write email addresses when people say them.		

Unit 4
My name's ...

Get ready to write

Carrie, a female exchange student is going to stay with Aiko in Tokyo. At the moment, Aiko does not know anything about her. She is waiting for an email from the student.

Carrie

Visit other countries with International Exchange

ARRIVALS

Aiko

- Write three questions Aiko wants the email to answer.
  a What ...?   (name)   What's her name?
  b Where ...?   (place)   _____
  c What ...?   (job/course) _____
- Write one other question that Aiko might ask.
  _____

go to Useful language p. 82

An email introducing yourself

Look at an example

1 **Look at the email Carrie sent to Aiko. Match topics a–e to paragraphs 1–5 in the email.**

   a herself ☐ 2
   b her hobbies ☐
   c her family ☐
   d her thanks ☐
   e how she feels about the exchange ☐

2 **Does Carrie answer all Aiko's questions from *Get ready to write*?**

Delete   Reply   Reply All   Forward   Print

From: Carrie Murphy
Date: 17 January
To: Aiko Watanabe
Subject: **My visit to Japan**

Dear Ms Watanabe

1 Thank you for being my 'host' in Japan. I'm really looking forward to staying with you!

2 My name is Carrie and I'm twenty-two years old. I come from Glengowrie, which is a suburb of Adelaide, and I'm studying nursing at the University. It's hard work but I have lots of fun.

3 At the weekend I like to go to concerts or go bowling with my friends from the University. I also enjoy taking my mum's dog to the Hazelmere Reserve for long walks.

4 I have two sisters and a brother called Bob. Wendy is younger than me and is still at high school and Tina is a dental nurse. We all grew up in another part of Adelaide called Parafield Gardens. Wendy and Tina still live there with my parents but Bob lives in Sydney now. We get on well but all sisters fight sometimes!

5 I am very excited about visiting Japan and meeting you because I love to travel and experience new things. I think it's going to be great!

Best regards

Carrie Murphy

Did you know ...?

Ms Watanabe   = title + surname
Ms A Watanabe   = title + initial + surname
Ms Aiko Watanabe   = title + first name + surname
                NOT Ms Aiko

1 Write your name in three different ways. Use the correct title (Ms, Miss, Mrs, Mr, Dr).

   a --
   b --
   c --

It is not always necessary to start an email with *Dear* and to end with *Best regards*. Carrie uses them because it is the first time she is writing to Aiko.

2 a Circle the phrases Carrie uses to start and end the email.
      Dear Aiko / Dear Ms Watanabe
      Best regards / Best wishes / Love
   b Which phrases can you write to a friend?
   c Which phrases can you write to someone you have not met?
      (See Appendix 7.)

3 **In her email, Carrie answers Aiko's questions. Write her answers.**

   a (Name) My name is Carrie. -----------------------
   b (Place) ---
   c (Job/course) ------------------------------------

4 **Now write the same information about yourself.**

   a (Name) ---
   b (Place) --
   c (Job/course) ------------------------------------

5 **Circle the statement that is correct for you.**

   a I have | no brothers or sisters. (I am an only child.)
           | one sister / brother.
           | two sisters / brothers.
           | (number) ...... sisters / brothers.

   b My parents | live in (place) ....
                 | aren't alive anymore.

   c I'm | single / divorced.
          | married.

   d I don't have any children.
      I have | one child.
             | two children.
             | (number) ...... children.

6 **This is how Carrie writes about her hobbies.**

   I like to go to concerts.   *I ... enjoy taking my Mum's dog ... for long walks ...*

   like to + verb + expression   *enjoy* verb*ing* + expression

   Write about your hobbies. Use the verbs and expressions below.

Verb +	**Expression**
go	to the cinema / to nice restaurants / to concerts / festivals
read	magazines / books
surf	the net
listen	to rock / to classical music / to pop / to jazz
watch	TV / movies
play	football / basketball / computer games
go	bowling / swimming

   a I like to --
   b I enjoy --

Focus on ...
sentences

[1]I have two sisters and a brother called Bob.
[2]Wendy is younger than me and still in high school.
[3]Tina is a dental nurse. [4]We all grew up in another part of Adelaide called Parafield Gardens.

1 Carrie has many things she wants to explain about her family. Match numbers 1–4 with headings a–d.
   a The size of the family [1]
   b Wendy ☐
   c Where they grew up ☐
   d Tina ☐

2 What is a sentence? Choose one of the words in brackets ( ) to complete these rules.
   a A sentence ____always____ contains one complete idea. (sometimes/always)
   b A full stop shows the reader where one idea _____ (finishes/begins).
   c A capital letter shows where the next idea _____ (finishes/begins).

3 Is this paragraph easy or difficult to understand? Why?
   i really like sport and listening to music i love karate i also enjoy going swimming at the leisure centre it's very near my house

4 In the paragraph, the reader doesn't know where ideas start and finish. It talks about four different things (my hobbies, my favourite hobby, another sport that I like, and where the leisure centre is).
   a Put a full stop where each idea finishes.
   b Put a capital letter where each new idea begins.

5 Write four sentences about your hobbies.

Plan

7 **Aiko is going on a student exchange to Germany. Her host is Lukas Reimers. Help Aiko to start and end an email to him. Use the *Did you know?* box on page 23 to help you.**

a Write the expression Aiko can use to start her email _____
b Write the expression she can use to end her email _____

8 **Look at Aiko's application form. Use information from the form to complete her sentences.**

a My name's Aiko. I come from _____ and I'm _____ years old.
b Complete this sentence for her about her hobbies.
At the weekend I like to _____
_____
c Write a sentence for her about her family.
_____
_____

International Student Exchange Programme

Complete this form and return it to ISEP, 22–25 McNaughton Road, Clayton, Victoria 3168 AUSTRALIA

Surname: _Watanabe_
First Name: _Aiko_
Address: _4-21-14 Soshigaya, Setagaya-ku, Tokyo, 157-0072, Japan_
Nationality: _Japanese_
Date of Birth: _7 July 1987_
Tel.: _0081 334 837231_
Email: _aiko@freecell.co.jp_
Languages Spoken: _Japanese, English, Portuguese_
Family: _no sisters or brothers, my parents live in Tokyo_
Country you want to visit: _Germany_
College/Work: _MBA, Tokyo University Business School_
Hobbies/interests: _techno music, nature, painting_

Signature: _A Watanabe_   Date: _6 August 2010_

Write

9 **Use the information from Plan to help Aiko write her email. Complete all the blanks.**

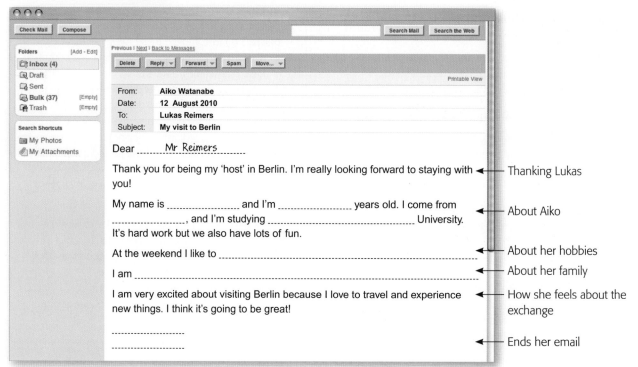

From: **Aiko Watanabe**
Date: **12 August 2010**
To: **Lukas Reimers**
Subject: **My visit to Berlin**

Dear __Mr Reimers__

Thank you for being my 'host' in Berlin. I'm really looking forward to staying with you! ◄—— Thanking Lukas

My name is _____ and I'm _____ years old. I come from _____, and I'm studying _____ University. It's hard work but we also have lots of fun. ◄—— About Aiko

At the weekend I like to _____ ◄—— About her hobbies

I am _____ ◄—— About her family

I am very excited about visiting Berlin because I love to travel and experience new things. I think it's going to be great! ◄—— How she feels about the exchange

_____
_____ ◄—— Ends her email

Check

- Have you written everything about Aiko that Lukas needs to know?
- Have you written in complete sentences?
- Have you used the correct title and name for Lukas?
- Have you used an appropriate expression to end the email?
- Have you written Aiko's name at the end of the email?

Learning tip

When you write, check
- Does the reader understand why I am writing to them?
- Are my ideas organized logically in sentences?

Did you answer 'yes' to both questions? Then check spelling and grammar.

Class bonus

Fold over the email you wrote for *Extra Practice* so no one can see your name. Display it on your classroom wall with your classmates' emails. Try to guess which email describes which person in your class.

Extra practice

Complete this form for yourself.

International Student Exchange Programme

Complete this form and return it to ISEP, 22–25 McNaughton Road, Clayton, Victoria 3168 AUSTRALIA

Surname: ....

First Name: ....

Address: ....

Nationality: ....

Date of Birth: ....

Tel.: ....

Email: ....

Languages Spoken: ....

Family: ....

Country you want to visit: ....

College/Work: ....

Hobbies/interests: ....

Signature: ....   Date: ....

- Carrie is going to be your host in Australia. Write an email introducing yourself.
- Ask your teacher or a native speaker to check that your email has all the information that Carrie needs.
- Ask them to check that you have used a new sentence for each new idea.

Can-do checklist

Tick what you can do.

	Can do	Need more practice
I can write an email introducing myself.		
I can write a description of my family and my hobbies.		
I can write the names and titles of people correctly in emails and letters.	✓	✓
I can use sentences correctly.		

Unit 5
Back at 6.00

Get ready to write

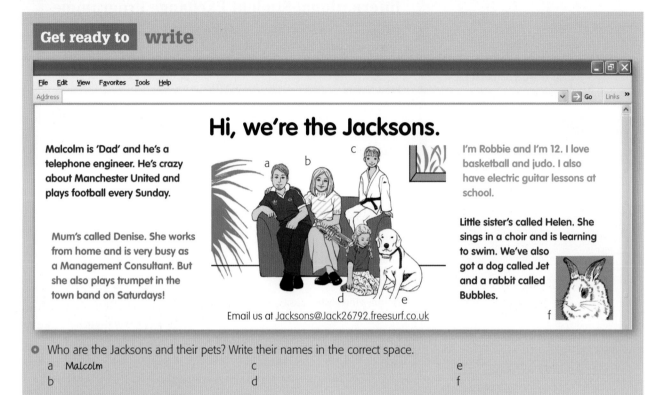

Hi, we're the Jacksons.

Malcolm is 'Dad' and he's a telephone engineer. He's crazy about Manchester United and plays football every Sunday.

Mum's called Denise. She works from home and is very busy as a Management Consultant. But she also plays trumpet in the town band on Saturdays!

I'm Robbie and I'm 12. I love basketball and judo. I also have electric guitar lessons at school.

Little sister's called Helen. She sings in a choir and is learning to swim. We've also got a dog called Jet and a rabbit called Bubbles.

Email us at Jacksons@Jack26792.freesurf.co.uk

- Who are the Jacksons and their pets? Write their names in the correct space.

  a Malcolm   c   e
  b   d   f

go to Useful language p. 82

A Leaving messages

Look at an example

1 The Jacksons often leave messages or notes for each other. Here are a few! Who do you think wrote each note? Who is the note to?

a Written by: ___Malcolm___ To: ___Denise___
b Written by: _____ To: _____
c Written by: _____ To: _____
d Written by: _____ To: _____
e Written by: _____ To: _____

2 Look at these statements about messages to your family and friends. Are they true (T) or false (F)?

a You don't have to write your full name. __T__
b You must write in complete sentences. _____
c You don't have to write pronouns (e.g. *I*) and auxiliary verbs (e.g. *am*). _____

a
Denise. At the pool with H. (Lesson's changed times.) Back at 6.00. M x

b
Robbie, Don't forget - feed Jet before basketball! Dad

c
Gone to the town centre. Meet me at the library at 2.00. M

d
Helen, Going to the park after Judo – want to come? Robbie

e
Mum, Gone to Paul's house. Can you pick me up at 4.00? Robbie

Plan

3 Cross out the words in these sentences that are not in the notes left by the Jacksons.

a ~~Do you~~ want to come?
b I've gone to the town centre.
c I'll be back at 6.00.
d I'm at the pool.

4 Match these expressions to the explanations.

a ~~Do you~~ want to …?
b Can you …?
c ~~I'll~~ see you / Meet me at *place* at *time*
d ~~I've~~ gone to … / ~~I'm~~ at …
e ~~I'll be~~ back / home before / at / after *time* / ~~I'll be~~ back / home in 15 minutes.

1 Asking the reader to do something
2 Inviting the reader to do something
3 Telling the reader when someone will return
4 Telling the reader where to meet
5 Telling the reader where someone is

Learning tip

– Always make your notes short. Then people will read them!
– Be careful! You normally leave a note if you can't speak to someone because they are out. When they read the note, they can't check anything that is confusing. Make sure you include all the important information.

5 You are staying with the Jacksons as a guest. They are out shopping. You want to go out but these things happen. Before you can go out you need to write some notes. Who do you write the different notes to?

a __Robbie__   b _____   c _____   d _____

a Robbie's friend, Paul, comes to the house. He says he's going swimming at 4.00. He wants Robbie to come. He says he'll wait at the bus stop for Robbie.

c You decide to have lunch at 1.00 at the pizzeria in town. You want to invite the Jacksons.

b The light in your room breaks. You want someone to fix it.

d Your friends phone and ask you to go to the cinema. The film finishes at 11.00.

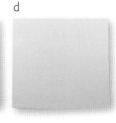

6 What expressions from Exercise 4 can you use in each note?

a Want to...? Meet him at the bus stop at 4.00
b _____
c _____
d _____

Write

7 Write the three notes.

a
Want to go swimming with Paul? Meet him at the bus stop at 4.00.

b

c

d

Check

– Does the reader know who the note is to?
– Does the reader know who the note is from?
– Is the message easy to understand?

Extra practice

– Think of your favourite hobby. Write a note to an English-speaking friend or your teacher inviting them to try your hobby. Include the time and place you should meet.
– Give your friend or teacher the note. Ask them to check to see if you have included all the information they need.

B Adding notes to a calendar

Look at an example

MARCH

Sunday	Monday	Tuesday	Wednesday	Thursday	Friday	Saturday
7	**8**	**9**	**10**	**11**	**12**	**13**
	H. swimming, 4.30–5.00		R. Guitar lesson, school	R. Basketball, Leisure Centre 4.00–6.00	H. choir 4.15–5.00, Town Hall	R. Judo 10.00–11.00, School D. Band 2.30–4.00, Town Hall

1 Look at one week from the Jackson's calendar. Look at the calendar entry for Thursday 11 March.

  a Who is doing something?   Robbie   c Where are they doing it?   ....

  b What are they doing?   ....   d When are they doing it?   ....

Plan

2 a Malcolm needs to put a note about his football practice on Sunday on the calendar. Cross out or shorten words to make this note shorter.

    Malcolm, football practice Leisure Centre between 11.00 and 1.00

  b Write his shorter note on the calendar above.

3 a Look at the calendar. What time does Helen go swimming?

    ....

  b 🔊 **9** Listen to this message on the Jacksons' telephone answering machine. The Leisure Centre want to change the time of the lesson. Write the new time.

    ....

4 Read this invitation and answer these questions.

  a Who is going to the party?   ....

  b Where is the party?   ....

  c When is the party?   ....

Dear Helen

it's my birthday!

Please come to my bowling party on Saturday 13 from 3.00–5.00 at the Leisure Centre.

Love
Sue

5 Read this dentist's appointment reminder and answer these questions.

  a Who is going to see the dentist?   ....

  b When are they going to see the dentist?   ....

Dental Appointment Reminder

Dear Mr Jackson
You are due for your dental check-up.
An appointment has been made for you on Tuesday 2 March at 5.30 Please phone to comfirm your appointment. Yours sincerely
Mr I Pullem BDS MFGDP
Salford Dental Surgery   reception@sdental.co.uk

Write

6 a Change the times of Helen's swimming lesson on this calendar.

   b Add new notes for the party and the dentist's appointment.

MARCH

Sunday	Monday	Tuesday	Wednesday	Thursday	Friday	Saturday
	1 H. swimming, 4.30–5.00	**2**	**3** R. Guitar lesson, school	**4** R. Basketball, Leisure Centre 4.00–6.00	**5** H. choir 4.15–5.00, Town Hall	**6** R. Judo 10.00–11.00, School D. Band 2.30–4.00, Town Hall
7 M. Football, 10.00–1.00 Leisure Centre	**8** H. swimming, 4.30–5.00	**9**	**10** R. Guitar lesson, school	**11** R. Basketball, Leisure Centre 4.00–6.00	**12** H. choir 4.15–5.00, Town Hall	**13** R. Judo 10.00–11.00, School D. Band 2.30–4.00, Town Hall

Check

– Have you used the initial of the person who is doing something?
– Have you written what they are doing?
– Have you written where they are doing it?
– Have you written the time they are doing it?

Class bonus

– In groups of three, talk about what you are going to do next week. After three minutes stop and work on your own.
– Draw a seven-day calendar. Try to remember everything that everyone is going to do next week. Add notes about these things to the calendar.
– When you are ready, swap your calendar with another student from your group. Read the other student's calendar and talk to them about anything they have forgotten or that is difficult to understand on their calendar.

E X tra practice

– Think about what you and your family are going to do next week. Add notes to this calendar to remind you.
– Use the check questions to check your notes.

Sunday	Monday	Tuesday	Wednesday	Thursday	Friday	Saturday

Can-do checklist

Tick what you can do.

	Can do	Need more practice
I can write short messages.	✔	✔
I can complete a calendar.	✔	✔

Get ready to write

- In the UK, people often send cards for special occasions like birthdays or weddings. Match the photographs to the cards.

  Photo a [2] Photo c [ ]
  Photo b [ ] Photo d [ ]

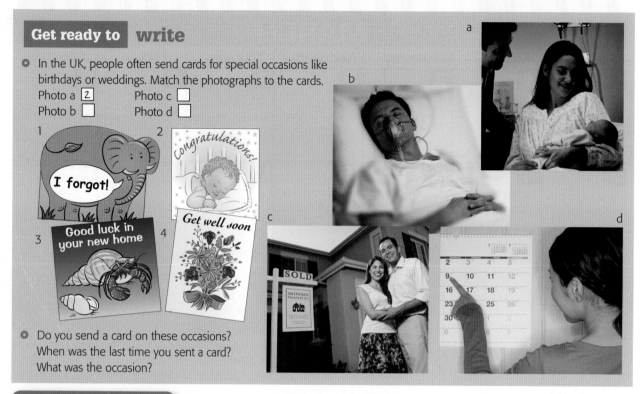

- Do you send a card on these occasions? When was the last time you sent a card? What was the occasion?

go to Useful language p. 83

A Messages in cards

Look at an example

1 Here are the messages in the cards. Were the people who wrote them happy or sad? Put a happy ☺ or sad face ☹ next to each message.

Plan

There are many ways to say that you want good things to happen.

Best wishes on/for your + **noun**

Best wishes | on your birthday.
| for your exams.

I hope you + **verb**

(I) hope you | have a wonderful day.
| do well in your exams.
| feel better soon.

Wishing you a + **adjective** + **noun**

Wishing you | a happy birthday.
| a quick recovery.

Good luck with/in your + **noun**

Good luck | with your exams.
| in your new home.

2 Complete these sentences.

a ....I hope you........ pass your driving test.
b .... with your driving test.
c .... a successful driving test.
d .... on your Wedding day.
e .... have a wonderful Wedding day.
f .... many happy years together.
g .... in your new job.

3 Your friend is getting married. What message can you write in her wedding card?

....
....

Write

4 Write a message to your friend in this wedding card.

Focus on ...
fixed expressions

Some expressions are fixed and do not change. Write them down and learn them as a single piece of new vocabulary. Look for words that always follow each other. For example 'Congratulations on . . .'

Complete these examples. Use expressions from Exercises 1 and 2.

Writing about things that make you happy ☺

a Happy | Christmas.
| Anniversary.
| New Year.
| Birthday ....

BUT ✗ Happy Wedding Day ✗
✓ Congratulations on your wedding. ✓

b Congratulations on | your engagement/anniversary.
| passing your driving test.
| getting your new job.
| your new home.
| ....

Writing about things that make you sad ☹

c (I'm) Sorry you're ill. Get well soon.
.... Hope you had a good day.

Check

– Have you written who the card is to?
– Have you written what good things you want to happen?
– Have you written something to end the message e.g. *Love*?
– Have you signed your name?

E✗tra practice

– A friend who works with you is getting a new job. Write him a message in this card.

– Use the **Check** questions to check your message.

B Thank you letters

Look at an example

1 Read the thank you letter that Stefano wrote and answer these questions.

a Who sent the camera?

----

b Was Stefano happy or unhappy with his present?

----

2 Are these statements true (T) or false (F)?

a Stefano writes the complete date. ..F..

b Stefano doesn't write his address because his Grandma knows it. ......

c Stefano writes *Dear Grandma* because it is more informal or friendly than *Hi Grandma*. ......

3 Put these in the same order as the thank you letter:

a Stefano says why he likes the present.

b Stefano writes something to end the letter.

c Stefano thanks the person who sent the present.

d Stefano says when he used the present.

e Stefano promises he will do something in the future.

Plan

4 What do these adjectives describe? Put the adjectives in the correct box. Some adjectives can go in more than one box.

a tasty b gorgeous c colourful d fun
e useful f enjoyable g interesting h trendy
i great j lovely

Food	Clothes	Books / DVDs
a		

25 June

Dear Grandma

Thank you for my birthday present. I've always wanted a good digital video camera and this one's excellent. I used it last night at my party and I've got lots of great shots of my friends pulling funny faces! Thanks very much!

I'll write again soon.

Lots of love
Stefano

5 Find ten adjectives that can describe different types of presents.

I	C	O	L	O	U	R	F	U	L	E
N	G	O	R	G	E	O	U	S	O	N
T	L	U	F	R	S	U	N	D	V	J
E	T	R	E	N	D	Y	G	H	E	O
R	T	A	S	T	Y	T	L	Y	L	Y
E	T	A	E	R	G	V	P	B	Y	A
S	B	J	P	S	U	G	M	W	X	B
T	D	N	V	V	Z	W	E	D	Z	L
I	P	E	G	R	E	A	T	O	R	E
N	L	K	Q	N	O	N	R	W	Q	Z
G	W	T	Q	Y	U	S	E	F	U	L

6 These people use their presents at different times. Write when: *in the past, now* or *in the future.*

a

> I used the camera at my party.

In the past.

b

> I'm wearing the t-shirt now.

....

c

> I'm going to read it tomorrow.

....

7 Look at the pictures of the presents people have sent you. Choose one present. Who sent it? ....

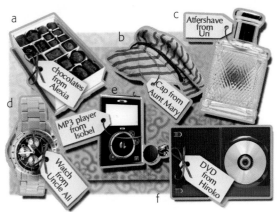

8 Choose an adjective from Exercise 5 to describe the present. ....

9 Choose when you use your present a, b or c.

a Are you using it now? ....
b Are you going to use it in the future? ....
c Did you use it in the past? ....

10 Look at Exercise 6. Write a sentence about when you use your present.

....

Write

11 Write a thank you letter for the present you chose in Exercise 7.

Check

– Have you written the date?
– Have you written who the letter is to?
– Have you written what the present is and why you like it?
– Have you written about when you use your present?
– Have you used an expression to end the letter, e.g. *Love*?
– Have you signed your name?

EX**tra practice**

– Write a thank you letter for the most unusual present you ever received.
– Use the **Check** questions to check it.

Can-do checklist

Tick what you can do.

	Can do	Need more practice
I can write cards for celebrations.	✔	✔
I can write about sad and happy occasions or events.		
I can write thank you letters.		

Unit 7
Let's party!

Get ready to write

Here are two places where people can have parties.

Think about these questions.
- Which place would you choose for your party? Why?
- Who would you invite?

go to Useful language p. 83

A An invitation

Look at an example

From: **Stef**
Date: **3 March**
To: **Isobel**
Subject: **It's my birthday!**

Hi!

I'm having a small celebration for my 18th birthday. I'd love it if you could join us. I've booked a table at an Italian restaurant called La Trattoria on Saturday 20th. We're all meeting there at 8.00 pm.

It's quite easy to find. Come out of the station and turn left. Go past the post office and go straight on for about 500m until you get to some traffic lights, go past them. La Trattoria is near the traffic lights. It's on the right, next to a small supermarket.

Please let me know ASAP if you can come! See you then?

Love
Stef

---

1 Look at the invitation. Write the answers to these questions.

a Who sent the invitation? _Stef_____
b What is the occasion? _____
c Where is it taking place? _____
d When is it taking place? _____

2 Stef includes directions to the restaurant. Why? Choose one of the answers from the list below.

a His friends probably haven't visited the restaurant before.
b His friends like Italian food.
c His friends don't know where he lives.

Did you know ...?

ASAP = as soon as possible (friendly and informal)
RSVP = Please reply (more polite and formal)
From French: répondez, s'il vous plaît

You can *accept* an invitation (phone or write to say *yes*) or you can *decline* an invitation (phone or write to say *no*). When you decline an invitation it is polite to say why you cannot go to the event, e.g. *I'm already going to a wedding on that day.*

3 How does the invitation ask Isobel to reply? Write the sentence it uses.

Plan

4 Isobel wants to have a party at her new house at 7.00 on 28 July. She wants to invite her friends. Answer these questions.

a What is the event? _A party_-------------------------
b Where is it? --
c When is it? --
d What other information does she need to include?
   ----

5 Look at these sentences from Stef's email.

I'm having a small celebration.
(The date of the celebration is fixed)
We're meeting there at 8.00.
(Stef told other people to meet at 8.00)

6 Complete this rule:

We use *to be* + _____ to talk about fixed plans and arrangements.

7 Complete two sentences Isobel can use about her party. Use *to be* + the verbs in brackets ( ).

a I _____ a party. (have)
b We _____ at 7.00. (eat)

Write

8 Help Isobel by writing the invitation to her party for her. Use this plan for the email.

Paragraph 1: Explain about the event.
Paragraph 2: Use the directions you wrote in **Focus on** directions.
Paragraph 3: Ask the person to reply.

Focus on ...
directions

1 Look at Isobel's directions below. Are they as helpful as Stef's directions on page 34?

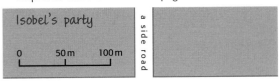

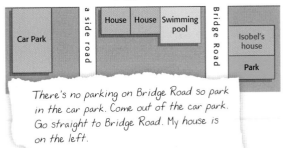

There's no parking on Bridge Road so park in the car park. Come out of the car park. Go straight to Bridge Road. My house is on the left.

2 Help Isobel give better directions. Here are some questions her friends might ask. Look at the map and answer them.
a When I leave the car park, which direction do I turn? _Right_____
b Do I go past anything? _____
c How far do I go? _____
d How do I know where Bridge Road is? Are there any big buildings near it? _____
e How do I know where you house is? Is there anything obvious near it? _____

3 Help Isobel by completing these improved directions.
   There's no parking on Bridge Road, so park in the car park. Come out of the car park and turn (a) _right__
   Go past the first (b) _____ *and go straight for about*
   (c) _____ *m. Bridge Road is* (d) _____ *the swimming pool. My house is on the left,* (e) _____ *to the park.*

Check

– Have you given all the necessary information about the event? What? Where? When?
– Have you written directions to Isobel's house?
– Have you asked for a reply?
– Have you written the date?
– Have you written what the 'Subject' of the email is?

E X tra practice

Write an email inviting friends from another town to a special meal at your favourite restaurant. Include the date and time of the meal and directions.

B A letter or email accepting or declining an invitation

Look at an example

a

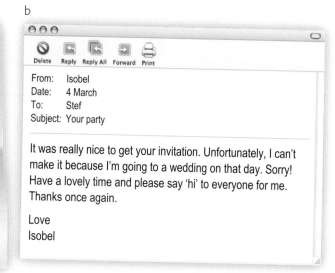

71 Bridge Road
Leeds
LE8 7DW

1st March

Dear Steven and Charlotte,

Thank you so much for the invitation to share your special day with you. I'll be very happy to come. I'm really looking forward to it.

Thank you once again.

Best wishes
Isobel Romero

b

From: Isobel
Date: 4 March
To: Stef
Subject: Your party

It was really nice to get your invitation. Unfortunately, I can't make it because I'm going to a wedding on that day. Sorry! Have a lovely time and please say 'hi' to everyone for me. Thanks once again.

Love
Isobel

1 Isobel has invitations to a wedding and a party. She cannot go to both. Which event does Isobel decide to go to?

----

2 What extra information does she include in the email?

----

3 Complete the gaps in this diagram with similar expressions from the letter and email.

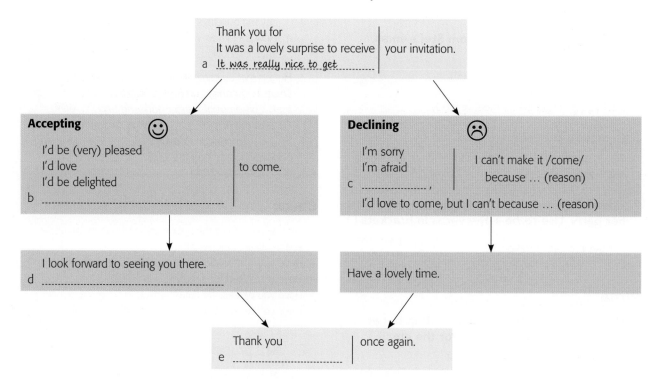

Thank you for
It was a lovely surprise to receive | your invitation.
a It was really nice to get

Accepting ☺

I'd be (very) pleased
I'd love | to come.
I'd be delighted
b ------------------------------------

Declining ☹

I'm sorry
I'm afraid | I can't make it /come/
c ------------------ ,   because ... (reason)

I'd love to come, but I can't because ... (reason)

I look forward to seeing you there.
d ------------------------------------

Have a lovely time.

Thank you | once again.
e ------------------------------

Focus on ...
explaining why you cannot do something

Because links two sentences. *Because* explains why the information in the first sentence is true.

I can't make it.   WHY?   **Because** *I'm going to a wedding on that day.*

I can't make it **because** *I'm going to a wedding on that day.*

1 Use because to link the sentences. Remember to use *to be + ing*.

a I'm sorry that I can't make it. I work on that day.

   I'm sorry I can't make it that day because I'm working.

b I'm afraid I can't come. I visit my parents on that day.

   ----

c Unfortunately, I can't come. I study for exams.

   ----

d I'd love to come, but I can't. I go on holiday.

Learning tip

English spelling can be difficult. Look for patterns. Sometimes pictures can help you remember difficult spellings. **Look**

b e c $\boxed{\text{a u s}}$ e
$\boxed{\text{A u s}}$ t r a l i a

Remember

be + c + $\boxed{\text{aus}}$ + e

Think of a spelling that you find difficult. Can you think of a word with a similar spelling pattern? In your mind, try to link them together in a picture.

Plan

4 Isobel has also asked you to go to her party. You are away on holiday with your family that week.

a Write a sentence to thank Isobel.

   ----

b Write a sentence declining the invitation.

   ----

5 Use the diagram from Exercise 1 to plan the rest of your reply. (Choose one sentence from each box.)

Write

6 Write your email to Isobel explaining why you cannot go.

Check

– Have you thanked Isobel for the invitation?
– If you've declined, have you given a reason?
– Have you written the date?
– Have you written what the 'Subject' of the email is?

Can-do checklist

Tick what you can do.

	Can do	Need more practice
I can write an invitation.	✓	✓
I can write a friendly and informal email accepting an invitation.		
I can write a friendly and informal email declining an invitation.		
I can use *because* to explain reasons.		
I can write about arrangements.		

Unit 8
Having a great time ...

Get ready to write

- 🔊 **10** Listen to some sounds from around the world, then match the sounds to the postcards.
  Sound 1 ___e___
  Sound 2 _____
  Sound 3 _____
  Sound 4 _____
  Sound 5 _____

Now think about these questions:
- Which place would you like to go to on holiday? Why?
- Do you send postcards when you go on holiday?
  Who do you send them to?
  What do you write about?

a   *The Great Wall*

c   *The Nile at Aswan*

b   *Belize*

The Greek Islands

d   *Beautiful Ireland*

e

go to Useful language p. 83

A postcard

Look at an example

1 Look at the postcards in *Get ready to write*. Which postcard do you think this is? Tick ✓ one.

a ☐
b ☐
c ☐
d ☐
e ☐

2 Match these questions to sentences in the postcard.

a What did you do yesterday? ☐3☐
b What are you going to do tomorrow? ☐
c What is the place like? What are the people like? ☐
d What is the weather like? ☐

Having a great time here in Ireland.
¹ Wonderful scenery and people very friendly!
² Weather's not too good but we've got umbrellas! ³Yesterday, went to the Puck Fair in Killorglin. It's a traditional festival and horse market. They crown a goat and make it king for three days. Lots of traditional music! Amazing! ⁴Tomorrow we're going to drive round the Ring of Kerry.
See you soon.
Lots of love
Sue and Pete

EIRE
4
Shamrock

Harriet Petrie
13 Nightingale Road
London
W1 6TM
ENGLAND

3 Are these 'rules' for writing postcards true (T) or false (F)?

a Always write *Dear*... __F__
b Always write your name or initials at the end. _____
c Always write the date. _____
d Do not write a closing remark, e.g. *Love from*. _____

Learning tip

You can write more than one page when you write a letter. You can use complete sentences because there is a lot of space. On a postcard, the space to write in is small. We make sentences shorter to fit the space.

pronoun + auxiliary verb

~~We are~~ having a great time here in Ireland.

You also do not write your address on a postcard.

4 **Look at the letter from Sue and Pete. Cross out anything that they do not include in their postcard, e.g.** ~~We are~~ **having a great time here in Ireland.**

Plan

> Lakeview Hotel
> Killarney, County Kerry
> Eire
>
> 12 August
>
> Dear Karen,
>   How are you? We are having a great time here in Ireland. There is wonderful scenery all round here and the people are very friendly! The weather's not too good but we've got our umbrellas!
>   Our journey took a long time: we drove down to Wales and caught a ferry to Rosslare. On the ferry we met a woman called Mary who told us about lots of places to visit.
>   Yesterday, we went to the Puck Fair in Killorglin. It's a traditional festival and horse market. They crown a goat and make it king for three days. Then they have a big party. What's great is that it isn't put on for the tourists, the people have been doing it for years and years. There is lots of traditional music! It's amazing!
>   Tomorrow we're going to drive round the Ring of Kerry. See you soon.
> Lots of love
> Sue and Pete

Focus on ...

giving your opinion (using *very*, *really*, *extremely* + adjectives)

The hotel is good. → The hotel is *very* good.

We use *very*, *really* and *extremely* to make most adjectives stronger.

BUT
The hotel is excellent. → ~~The hotel is very excellent.~~ ✗
                         The hotel is really excellent. ✓

Excellent = 100% good.
You cannot use *very* or *extremely* to make 100% adjectives stronger.
Use *really* to make 100% adjectives stronger.

1 Are these 100% adjectives positive (+) or negative (−)?
   a great +   b awful   c terrible   d fantastic
   e excellent   f amazing   g disgusting

2 Are these sentences correct ✓ or incorrect ✗?
   a The flight was very great. ✗
   b The Great Wall of China is really amazing.
   c The scenery in Ireland is extremely fantastic.
   d The weather in the rainforest is very bad.

3 What do you think? Use *very*, *really* or *extremely* + one of the adjectives in brackets ( ).
   a Travelling is ___very good___ (good/bad)
   b Beijing is _____ (busy/quiet)
   c Beach hotels are _____ (awful/fantastic)
   d Old ruins are _____ (boring/interesting)
   e People in most countries are _____ to tourists. (nice/rude)

4 What do you think? Complete these sentences. Use *very*, *really* or *extremely* + an adjective.
   a Traditional music is _____
   b City holidays are _____
   c Festivals are _____
   d Watching the sun set over the sea is _____

Did you know ...?

When English people write a postcard, they want the reader to think about how good the holiday is. When something is bad they try to make it sound better. They use *not too*.

~~The weather's bad.~~

The weather's not too good.

(not too good = bad)

Learning tip

Some words are very difficult to spell. Make funny sentences from the letters to help you remember.

Bill
eats
anything.
Unfortunately,
that
includes
Francine's
umbrella.
Lovely!

Oh, no!

Now make a funny sentence to help you spell one of these words: *necessary, friend, science*.

Look at some of your written work and find a word that your teacher always corrects. Make a funny sentence from its letters. Learn the sentence. You won't spell the word incorrectly again!

5 Make these bad things sound better. Use *not too* + adjective. Look at the *Did you know?* box to help you.

a The sea is cold. *The sea isn't too hot.*
b The museum was boring. ....
c The food is horrible. ....

6 Mary and Adam are on holiday in Egypt. They want to write a postcard. Help them to make the letter shorter.

a Cross out anything that is not normally included in a postcard, e.g. the address.
b Cross out anything that will not interest the reader.
c Cross out any unnecessary pronouns and auxiliary verbs.
d Make the underlined adjectives stronger or more positive e.g. good → very good.
e Make the circled adjective sound better, e.g. bad → not too good.

Old Cataract Hotel
Aswan, Egypt

25 January

Dear Carly,

I hope you're okay. We're in Aswan at the moment and are having a good holiday. It's a bit hot but the hotel is okay. It's about a hundred years old and there are views over the Nile with the desert in the background. Lots of little white sailing boats called feluccas go from one side of the river to the other, stopping at the islands. This morning we caught a felucca from the hotel steps to Kitchener's Island. It's a big Botanical Garden with trees with long spikes on their trunks! We walked across the Island and got back on the felucca at the other end. At Elephantine Island we saw the Nilometer (the thing the ancient Egyptians used to see how high the water was). We also visited the Museum which was boring but had a few mummies in the basement. In the afternoon we went to the bazaar. It's exotic and has lots of little shops selling spices, game boards and rugs. I didn't buy anything but it was good for window shopping! I think I'll go back another day. Tomorrow we're going on an excursion to see the massive temples at Abu Simbel. The coach leaves at 4.00 in the morning! I hope I get up on time.

We'll talk to you when we get back.

Lots of love
Mary (and Adam)

Write

7 Use the shortened letter to write Mary and Adam's postcard.

Carly MacKay

13 Pilrig Street,

Edinburgh

EH9 7JK

UNITED KINGDOM

Check

- Have you explained where Mary and Adam are?
- Have you explained what the place, hotel or weather is like?
- Have you explained what they have done and what they are going to do?
- Have you explained how Mary and Adam feel about their holiday?
- Have you used adjectives + *very, quite, extremely, not too* to make it more interesting?
- Have you cut any unnecessary information?
- Have you cut any unnecessary pronouns and auxiliary verbs?

E tra practice

- Think about your dream holiday or use one of the other postcards.
- Find out more about the place by searching www.google.com
- Complete the boxes.

Place	
Things you can do there	
Why is it special?	

- Imagine you are on holiday in the place and write a postcard to an English-speaking friend.

Can-do checklist

Tick what you can do.

	Can do	Need more practice
I can write a postcard.	✔	✔
I can express opinions.		
I can make bad things sound better than they are.		

Unit 9
How are you?

go to Useful language p. 83

Get ready to write

Look at the photo and think about these questions:

- Where is Luis?
- What is he doing?
- Do you think he lives in that country?

Luis

A personal letter
Look at an example

Mrs I Martinez
116 Deerfield Street
Boston MA 02215-1803

C/O Mr and Mrs Spencer
215 East 86th Street ← Writer's address
New York NY 10028-1208

1 August ← Date

Greeting → Dear Aunt Isidro,

Beginning the letter → Guess what? I'm in the US! I can't believe it...New York is
wonderful and I'm staying for a whole two weeks studying English.
My host family is great so I should improve. Sometimes they speak
very fast but most of the time I understand them. They've got a
son called Marcus who's crazy! He's 17 and is a brilliant baseball
player. He's taught me a lot already.

How are you? How's your job going? Do you get much free time?

After the course I plan to travel a little around the East Coast
(especially Boston). I'd love to drop in on you if you'd like me to.
What do you think? Write to me care of Mr and Mrs Spencer.

Ending the letter → Hope to see you soon.

All the best ← Saying goodbye

Writer's name → Luis

1 a Who is Luis writing to?

---

b What is he going to do?

---

c What does he want his aunt to do?

---

2 <u>Underline</u> the rules for personal letters and emails.

a <u>Use friendly, spoken English.</u> / Use more polite and formal English.

b Use contractions, e.g. *can't.* / Never use contractions.

c Use first names only, e.g. Peter. / Use complete names, e.g. Peter Applegarth.

3 Look at the address at the top of the letter. What does Luis write to show that Mr and Mrs Spencer will pass letters to him?

Did you know ...?

Greeting	Dear Jane / Dear Mum / Hi Jane
	Dear Jane$_{,}$ Comma or no punctuation. Dear Jane$_{,}$
	NOT Dear Jane$_{!}$
Beginning	Guess what? (+ write your news)
	How are you? (+ ask for news)
	I hope you're okay.
Ending	Hope to hear from you soon. / Write soon. / Please write!
Saying goodbye	All the best / Best wishes (to friends)
	Love / Lots of love (to family / boyfriend /
	very close friends)
	NOT Goodbye!

Learning tip

– When you read something in English look at how it is organized. Think about what each paragraph is about. Try to decide why the writer organized the writing in that way.

– Start a new paragraph every time you change the subject in your own writing.

Focus on ...
paragraphs

Paragraphs help the reader to understand where one subject finishes and a new one begins.

Look at this part of the letter. Luis starts a new paragraph to show he is writing about a new subject.

> *brilliant baseball player. He's taught me a lot already.*
>
>   *How are you? How's your job going? Do you get much free time?*

There are two ways for a writer to start a new paragraph.

a Personal letters
- Start a new line.
- Start writing about 2 cm from the edge of the other writing.

Example:

> *brilliant baseball player. He's taught me a lot already.*
>
> <u>2 cm</u>→ *How are you? How's your job going? Do you get much free time?*

b Email and business letters
- Leave a line space.
- Start writing directly under the other writing.

Example:

> *brilliant baseball player. He's taught me a lot already.*
> ↕
> *How are you? How's your job going? Do you get much free time?*

1 a Read this section of a personal letter. Use $\}$ to mark where a new paragraph should start.

> *While I was in Boston I went to a really good restaurant that had excellent pasta. Next week I start work again. I'm not looking forward to it!*

b Rewrite the section of the letter from Exercise 1a. Show where the new paragraph begins.

2 Imagine you are writing to a friend who you have not written to for many years. Write two short paragraphs. In paragraph 1 write the most important thing you did last year. In paragraph 2 write what you plan to do next year.

Focus on ...
writing addresses on envelopes

1 Look at how Luis wrote Aunt Isidro's address on the envelope on page 42. Are these statements true (T) or false (F)?
   a He uses commas (,) and full stops (.). ..F..
   b He uses capital letters. ......
   c All the lines start in the same place. ......

2 Put / at the start of each new line in these addresses.
   Example: Stefano Rossi / 116 Deerfield Street / Boston MA 02215-1803
   a Peter Applegarth 11 St Leonards Place YORK YO9 7ET
   b Suzie Edwards 802 Font Boulevard San Francisco CA 94132-4036

3 Write this address on the envelope.
   Mr J Bomberg 153 Mountbatten Avenue Ottawa ON K1H 5V6 Canada

BY AIR MAIL
par avion
Royal Mail
64p

Plan

4 Soren Hedegaard is Luis's classmate from the language school in New York. He is still studying there but Luis is back in Spain after visiting Boston. Luis wants to write to him. What can Luis ask Soren about? Write one question.

   ----

5 Look at Luis's letter on page 45. He has asked an English-speaking friend to check it for him. His friend has marked where he needs to add things ^. Match the number in the letter to the thing he needs to add.
   a an opening [2]
      e.g. *How are you?*
   b his address [ ]
      Av de la Albufera, 161
      28038 Madrid
      Spain
   c saying goodbye [ ]
      e.g. *All the best*

Did you know ...?

In some countries you write information on different lines on the envelope.

US, Australia and Canada
Name of person
Street number and name
Town or city + STATE ABBREVIATION,
e.g. *MA* (for the state of 'Massachusetts')
+ post / zip code

UK
Name of person
Street number and name
TOWN or CITY

POST CODE

On international post write the COUNTRY on a new line at the bottom of the address.

Use capital letters for this information.

For information about other countries visit the Universal Postal Union website: http://www.upu.int/post_code/en/postal_addressing_systems_member_countries.shtml

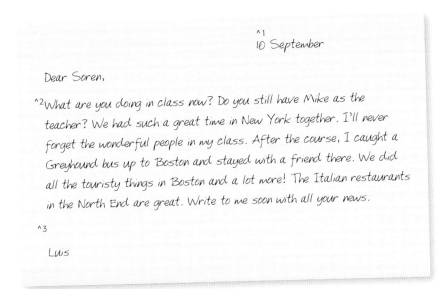

^1
10 September

Dear Soren,

^2What are you doing in class now? Do you still have Mike as the teacher? We had such a great time in New York together. I'll never forget the wonderful people in my class. After the course, I caught a Greyhound bus up to Boston and stayed with a friend there. We did all the touristy things in Boston and a lot more! The Italian restaurants in the North End are great. Write to me soon with all your news.

^3

Luis

Check

The envelope
– Is it easy to read?
– Do all the lines start in the same place?
– Have you cut all punctuation?
– Have you used capital letters in the correct place?
– Have you used C/O to show the language school should pass on the letter?

The letter
– Does it make sense?
– Have you used paragraphs to show where you change the subject?
– Have you included all the sections from **Look at an example**?

6 Look at the letter. Luis has not written in paragraphs. Find where he asks for news, writes his news, and closes the letter. Use ⌐ to mark where new paragraphs should start.

Write

7 Luis wants the New York school to pass the letter to Soren. Help Luis by addressing the envelope. The school's address is Campbell Language School, 537 Argyle Rd, Brooklyn, NY 11230-1510 USA.

EXtra practice

– Imagine Suzie Edwards is your pen friend (US: pen pal). Write a letter to her about what you have done recently and ask about her news.
– Address an envelope. Her address is 802 Font Boulevard, San Francisco CA 94132-4036 USA.
– Use the **Check** questions to help you check your letter and envelope.
– If you do not have a pen pal already, go to a pen pal website (e.g. www.iecc.org) and get one!

8 Rewrite Luis's letter using paragraphs.

Can-do checklist

Tick what you can do.

	Can do	Need more practice
I can write personal letters.	✓	✓
I can address envelopes correctly.		
I can use paragraphs correctly.		

Review 1
Social and travel

A Planning your writing

Choosing what to write

1 You are at home on your own. You are going out. You want to tell someone that you will be late home. What do you do?

  a complete a form b write a note
  c write a personal letter or email d write a card

2 It's a friend's birthday. What do you do?

  a complete a form b write a note c write a postcard
  d write a card

3 You need to send a parcel to another country. What do you do?

  a complete a form
  b write a note
  c write a personal letter or email
  d write a card

4 You want to send a friend detailed directions to your house. What do you do?

  a complete a form b write a postcard
  c write a personal letter or email d write a note

Knowing the reader

5 You are writing an email to your boyfriend or girlfriend. What style will you use? Choose one.

  a friendly and informal (e.g. *Guess what?*)
  b more polite and formal (e.g. *You will be surprised to hear …*)

6 You are writing a letter to someone you do not know. What style will you use? Choose one.

  a friendly and informal (e.g. *Guess what?*)
  b more polite and formal (e.g. *You will be surprised to hear …*)

Choosing information

7 Which of these is the most important information to include in an email introducing yourself?

  a your name b your mother's name
  c your date of birth d where you live

8 Which of these do you probably not need to include in a letter to a friend?

  a your address b how you are
  c news about your job d your plans

9 What do you think you would put in the contact details on a bank form?

  a Your address
  b Your nationality
  c How much money you are paid
  d Your job

B Checking your writing

Checking that the reader has enough information

10 Read this note. What information is missing that the reader needs to know?

  Dad. Gone to Suzi's house. Can you pick me up? Carla
  a Who? b Where? c What? d When?

11 Read this invitation. What information is missing that the reader needs to know?

  Dear Marlene, Please come to my party on 30th June at 6.30. Love Freda
  a Who? b Where? c What? d When?

12 Read this entry on a family's calendar. What information could be cut?

Wednesday	Thursday	Friday
	a Peter	
	b Drama club	
	c 7.30–9.30	
	d Rehearsing a play	

Checking that the information is well organized

13 Decide which sentence best explains why Chien-nien does not want to go to Paris.

a   I don't want to go to France next week and I'm visiting my uncle.

b   I don't want to go to France because I'm visiting my uncle.

c   I don't want to go to France. Because I'm visiting my uncle.

d   Because I don't want to go to France next week and I'm visiting my uncle.

14 David is writing to say he cannot go to a party. In which paragraph is the information organized best?

a   I've recently got a job as a night club doorman. They asked me last week if I could work that night. I didn't know you were having a party, so I said 'yes'. I'm sorry that I can't come to your party.

b   They asked me last week if I could work that night. I've recently got a job as a night club doorman. I didn't know you were having a party, so I said 'yes'. I'm sorry that I can't come to your party.

c   I'm sorry that I can't come to your party. I've recently got a job as a night club doorman. They asked me last week if I could work that night. I didn't know you were having a party, so I said 'yes'.

15 Simone is writing an email to a friend. She is giving her news. Look at where the paragraphs start and finish. Which is organized best?

a
> I had a great holiday in Thailand. The food was brilliant and the people so friendly.
>
> I'd recommend it as a place to go. My sister's now studying at college in America. She'll be back for Christmas though.

b
> I had a great holiday in Thailand. The food was brilliant and the people so friendly. I'd recommend it as a place to go.
>
> My sister's now studying at college in America. She'll be back for Christmas though.

c
> I had a great holiday in Thailand.
>
> The food was brilliant and the people so friendly. I'd recommend it as a place to go. My sister's now studying at college in America. She'll be back for Christmas though.

d
> I had a great holiday in Thailand. The food was brilliant and the people so friendly. I'd recommend it as a place to go. My sister's now studying at college in America.
>
> She'll be back for Christmas though.

Checking layout and style

16 **Simone has written her friend's address on the envelope. Which addressed envelope is best?**

17 **This is Simone's letter to her friend. Look at the details below the letter and decide where Simone should put them in the letter.**

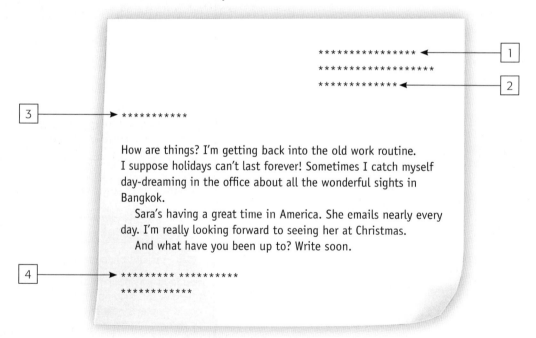

How are things? I'm getting back into the old work routine. I suppose holidays can't last forever! Sometimes I catch myself day-dreaming in the office about all the wonderful sights in Bangkok.

Sara's having a great time in America. She emails nearly every day. I'm really looking forward to seeing her at Christmas.

And what have you been up to? Write soon.

a 12 November 2010
b 11 Greenfield Avenue / Cambridge / CB16 1 DX
c Love / Her signature
d Dear Marta

18 **Simone is writing in England on 12 November 2010. What is the other correct way she can write the date?**

a 12/11/10 b 11/12/10 c 10/11/12 d 10/12/11

19 **You are taking part in a student exchange programme. You know the name of the person you are writing to but have never met them. How can you start your email?**

a Dear Kenzo b Dear Mr Asaki
c Dear Sir d Hi

Checking punctuation

20–22 Look at these sentences. A full stop is missing. Where should it be? Choose a, b, c or d for each sentence.

20 I have been in this country ^a for five years ^b it is a wonderful country ^c and I like it ^d very much.

21 I want to sell ^a my mountain bike ^b I have had it for five years ^c but I haven't used it much ^d because I don't enjoy cycling.

22 We can go swimming, ^a we can also play basketball ^b, football ^c and squash ^d if you like.

Checking grammar

23–24 One sentence for each question is correct. Choose the correct sentence.

23 a I enjoy going to the cinema.
    b I like go to the cinema.
    c I enjoy going cinema.
    d I enjoy go to the cinema.

24 a My English class is very excellent!
    b My English class is really excellent.
    c My English class is extremely excellent.
    d My English class is very awful!

25 **You planned a party and told some of your friends about it. You forgot to invite one person. You are now emailing them. What do you write?**
    a I am having a small party on Wednesday.
    b I have a small party on Wednesday.
    c I having a small party on Wednesday.
    d I will a small party on Wednesday.

Checking capital letters

26–28 Look at these sentences. Which word needs a capital letter?

26 My ^aname is Marek Pater and I ^bcome from a small ^ctown in ^dpoland.

27 I have been ^alearning ^benglish for ^cfive ^dyears.

28 My ^abirthday is on a ^bwednesday ^cthis ^dyear.

29 **Look at this sentence. Which word does not need a capital letter?**

^aI stayed in ^bNew Zealand in ^cMarch last ^dYear and had a great time.

Checking vocabulary

30 **Improve these sentences. Replace the underlined words with a word (or words) from the list on the right.**
    a I want a two bed room.   single / twin/ double / family
    b I work 9.00 until 5.00.   part time / self-employed / full time / employed
    c Paris is very nice.   awful / fantastic / terrible / disgusting

31 **You are completing a form. Which of these is a post code?**
    a Tel: 01604 6577665
    b psmall@hotmail.com
    c 29 Chester Road
    d SG8 7NN

32 **Which expression is incorrect?**
    a Congratulations on Christmas.
    b Happy Anniversary.
    c Happy Birthday.
    d Congratulations on passing your examinations.

Checking spelling

33–36 Which word is spelt correctly in each list?

33 a beautiful   b beautifull   c beatiful   d beutiful

34 a addres   b address   c adres   d adress

35 a enployed   b emploied   c employd   d employed

36 a becos   b becose   c because   d becase

Unit 10
Timetables

Get ready to write

- Monique Bernard is starting her course at the New Hope School, Capetown. She wants to talk to people at the school about two different things. Which two people should she talk to?
  - a Lesley Smith
  - b Barnie Peters
  - c Ulrike Orback
  - d Mel Merino

go to Useful language p. 83

A Notes about classes

Look at an example

First day timetable

9.00–9.30	Welcome talk – Lesley Smith (Student Lounge)
9.30–10.30	Test (Rm. 1)
11.00–11.15	Break
11.15–12.00	Tour of the school (meet in the cafeteria)
12.00–12.15	Talk: Living in South Africa – Ulrike (Student Lounge)
12.15–12.30	Talk: What's on – Barnie (Student Lounge)
12.30–13.30	Lunch

Did you know …?

A *tutor* teaches one student or a small class in a college or university. A *lecturer* talks to a larger group of students about a subject. This talk is called a *lecture*.

1 Look at Monique's timetable for her first day.
  Use information from the timetable to complete this chart.

When?	9.00–9.30	9.30–10.30	11.00–11.15	12.00–12.15	12.15–12.30
What?	Welcome talk		Break		
Who?	Lesley Smith	–	–		
Where?	Student Lounge		Cafeteria		

2 a When can Monique thank someone for choosing a good host family for her? _____

  b When can she talk to someone about visiting Table Mountain? _____

3 What is a short way of writing the word *room* on a timetable? _____

Plan

Class Lists (continued)

General English, Intermediate, Room 1
9.00–10.30, Tutor: Mel
11.00–12.30, Tutor: Helen

Monique Bernard
Wang Chien-nien
Jan Liden
Lene Moller
Ryozo Otsuji
Miroslav Sawicki
Brigitte Schmidt
Salaheddine El Yazghi

Individual lessons (15.00–16.30) Fridays
Gerhard Platter   Teacher: Mel   Room 7
Yuriko Murakami   Teacher: Helen   Room 9
Monique Bernard   Teacher: Richard   Room 8

Special Subjects
Special subjects are taught in the afternoon
(13.30–15.00). Choose one from each list.

Mondays and Wednesdays
Writing: Learn to write emails and letters with
David in Room 10.
Vocabulary: Practise new words in context.
(Mel, Room 5)
Tradition and Culture: Learn about the life and
history of the Southern African peoples.
(Richard, Room 2)

Tuesdays and Thursdays
English through song: Enjoy the latest songs and
learn English! (Helen, Room 7)
Listening and Speaking: Practise your speaking
and listening with David in Room 6.
Business: Learn how to communicate in business.
(Kate, Room 1)

Lectures – July
All lectures take place in the Student Lounge.

4 July   World English: a changing language in the 21st century – Dr C Glass
11 July   The history of rock music – Steve Wroe
18 July   South Africa: its history and future – Lesley Smith
25 July   The environment: Global Warming or global warning? – Solomon Porritt

4 Circle the information that is important for Monique on the class list.
e.g. Room 1

5 Look at the Special Subjects. Monique thinks she needs to learn more English words and how to speak English for her job. Underline the subjects that would be good for her.
e.g. Writing

6 Look at the titles of the lectures. Cross out anything that does not help you remember the main subject of the lecture.
e.g. World English: a changing language in the 21st century – Dr. C Glass

7 Choose a maximum of three words that explain the subject of the lecture.
a World English: a changing language in the 21st century
World English
b The history of rock music
c South Africa: its history and future
d The environment: Global Warming or global warning?

8 Monique is studying from 7 to 11 July. Which lecture can she attend?

51

Write

9 Monique decided to take the Vocabulary and Listening and Speaking Special Subjects. Help her complete her timetable. Add important information about her classes and notes to remind her about the lecture.

7–11 July	Monday	Tuesday	Wednesday	Thursday	Friday
9.00–10.30	General English	General English	General English	General English	General English
11.00–12.30	General English	General English	General English	General English	General English
12.30–13.30	Lunch				
13.30–15.00					Lecture
15.00–16.30					

Check

– Can you understand your notes?
– Have you written where the classes take place?
– Have you written who the teachers are for each class?
– Have you written the name of any special subjects or lectures?

E✗tra practice

– Think about the perfect English course for you. Choose four subjects you want to focus on, e.g. grammar, pronunciation, speaking and listening, vocabulary, reading, writing etc. Think about how much time you would like to spend studying each subject.
– Think about any special subjects you want to have in the afternoons or any lectures you would like.
– Think about the best teachers you have had in the past. Decide which classes they will teach on your perfect course.
– Write the timetable.
– Use the **Check** questions to make sure you have included all the important information in the timetable.

B Notes about assignments

Look at an example

1 The New Hope School has a test for all students every month. What information do you think Monique wants to find out from her teacher? e.g. What does the test include?

----

2 (11) Listen to Monique's teacher telling her class about the test. Does she give all the information Monique needs?

----

3 Listen again. These are Monique's notes. One thing is incorrect. Can you correct it?

Test
– Monday, 10.00
– Room 1
– Met Helen
– 40 multiple choice questions
– email/letter
– no dictionaries/translators
– no speaking/listening test

4 Are these statements true (T) or false (F)?

a Monique circled 'Test' because it helps her understand what the notes are about. It is a summary. ..T..

b She put the information in a list. The things the teacher says first are at the top of the list. The things the teacher says last are at the bottom of the list. ......

c She wrote the day and time at the top of her list because it is the most important information. ......

Learning tip

When you write short notes about homework, write each piece of information on a new line.
Check that your notes answer these questions. *What? When? Is there anything extra I need to know?*
If your notes do not answer these questions, ask the teacher to explain the homework again!

Plan

5 You are in Monique's class. The teacher is going to tell you about homework. What do you need to know?

----

6 Part of the homework is to find some information. How do you think the teacher will help you?

----

7 Write three questions you want the teacher to answer.

Write

8 a 🔊12 Listen to your teacher and write notes about your homework.

Homework
Essay
Title:

Look at: 1.
              2.

b (Circle) what the notes are about. (If you are not sure about what to do, look at Exercise 3 again.)

c <u>Underline</u> the title of the essay.

Check

– Can you understand your notes?
– Have you made a note of the title?
– Have you made a note of when you must do the homework by?
– Have you made a note of useful books or websites?

E✗tra practice

– 🔊13 Barnie is organising a trip. Your teacher wants you to do some preparation for it. Listen and write notes.
– Use the **Check** questions to check your notes.

Can-do checklist

Tick what you can do.

	Can do	Need more practice
I can transfer notes about classes onto a timetable.	✓	✓
I can write down notes about homework when a teacher explains.		

Unit 11
Wanted

Get ready to write

- Imagine you are a student studying in a different country for a year. Think about these questions:
  a Which bicycle will you buy? Why?
  b Where can you find advertisements for second-hand things in your country?
  In shop windows ☐
  In newspapers ☐
  On the Internet ☐

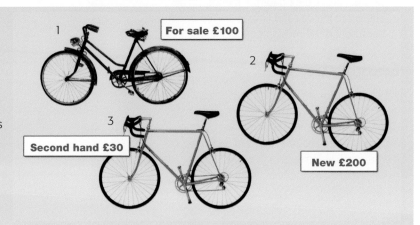

1 For sale £100

2 New £200

3 Second hand £30

go to Useful language p. 83

A Short advertisements for an intranet

Look at an example

http://www.roystoncollege.com/studentnotices

Royston College

| Welfare & Accommodation | Academic Support | Recreation | Student services |

Student notices

Law book for sale – bargain
Dictionary of International Law, 3rd edition. Very good condition. It costs a lot in the shops. I'm selling it for only £10 (or nearest offer) because I'm going home to Korea and can't carry it! Email Hei at hp234@ur.ac.uk or phone 01763 246098 (evenings).

Turkish language teacher wanted
I'm an English student looking for Turkish language tuition. I have some basic knowledge of grammar and vocab. I'm happy to negotiate a price. Contact Steve at sp1087@ur.ac.uk

Japanese to English translation wanted
I have a scientific paper that was published in Japan. I will pay £50 for someone to translate it for me. For more details, or to see the paper, please email Trisha at tr2456@ur.ac.uk

The college does not accept any liability for any products or services advertised on this website.

1 **Look at the web page for students at Royston College. Answer these questions.**

a Who wants to sell something?
..... Hei .....
b Who wants to learn something?
....
c Who wants to pay for something
....

2 **Are these statements true (T) or false (F)?**

a The advertisements use friendly and informal English. ...T...
b The advertisements are written in complete sentences. ......
c Each advertisement has a short title. ......
d The advertisers have put their email addresses because the advertisements are on a web page. ......

3 **Put these in the order they are written in the advertisements.**

a the person to contact ☐
b the price (or payment) ☐
c extra information ☐
d how to contact the person ☐
e the thing that is wanted or for sale ☐1

Plan

4 These expressions describe how good a thing is. Put them in the correct box. You can put more than one phrase in some boxes.

a as new   b brand new   c hardly used
d nearly new   e used once   f very good condition
g reasonable condition   h may need some repair

Second-hand				New
Poor	okay	good	excellent	
			a	

5 These expressions explain why you want to sell something. Match them to the explanations.

a Unwanted present.
b No longer needed.
c Duplicate.

1 I don't need it anymore.
2 I have two.
3 Someone gave it to me and I don't like it.

6 *I'm happy to/willing to negotiate a price.* What does this sentence mean? Choose one answer.

a I want to contact you and agree the price with you.
b You must tell me the price.
c I will tell you the price.

Did you know …?

An *intranet* is the computer network of a company or college. Only people who work in the company or study at the college can use the company or college's intranet.

7 You are leaving college. You own a Sony 750W Microwave oven. You bought it a year ago. It cost £100. You want to sell it for about £50. Complete this information.

a Title for the advertisement For sale – Microwave oven
b Extra information
   Details, e.g. Make, Type etc. _____
   _____
   Condition _____
   Reason for selling _____
   Cost _____
c Price _____
d Your name _____
e How to contact you _____
   _____

8 Complete these advertisements. Use sentences from the box below.

a **Room wanted**
   I need a room in a student house.
   I'm happy to negotiate the rent per month.
   Contact Sue at sg103@ur.ac.uk.
b **First year books needed**
   I want first year American Literature books.
   _____
   Phone Tom on 01763 256874.
c **Language exchange**
   I'm looking for someone to practise my English with.
   _____
   Email Thierry at th870@ur.ac.uk

> I'm happy to negotiate the rent per month.
> In exchange, I will teach you French.
> I will pay £20.

9 You want to go to London for the weekend, travelling on Friday 12 October. You want to know if any other students are planning to go to London on that day. You will only have one small backpack with you and want to share a car. You are willing to pay some of the cost of petrol. Complete the information.

a Title for the advertisement Car-share wanted
b What you want _____
   _____
c Extra information: Luggage _____
   _____
d What you will do in exchange _____
   _____
e Your name _____
   _____
f How to contact you _____
   _____

Learning tip

Difficult words may be part of a family of words. First learn how to spell the smallest word in the family. It will help you with the others!

Thing (short form):	*an*	advert
Verb:	*to*	advertise (something)
Person:	*an*	advertiser
Thing (long form)	*an*	advertisement

Write

10 Look at Exercises 7 and 9. Write the advertisement for either the microwave or the car share. Use complete sentences.

Check

– Imagine you are reading the advertisement for the first time. Does it give all the information you need?
– Does your title explain what you want or what you are selling?
– Have you included all the important extra information?
– Does the reader know who to contact?
– Does the reader know how to contact the advertiser?
– Have you written in complete sentences?

E✗tra practice

– Think of one thing that you own but do not want anymore. What is it? Is there anything special about it? What condition is it in? How much do you want to sell it for? Write the advertisement to go on an intranet.
– Think of one thing that you need for your English studies. What is it? How much do you want to pay for it? Write the advertisement to go on an intranet.
– Use the **Check** questions to check your advertisements.
– Ask your teacher or a native speaker to check that they understand your advertisements.

B Short advertisements for a notice board

Look at an example

1 Look at this notice board on a wall at Royston College. Students can use it to advertise things they need or want to sell. Think about how these advertisements are different to those on the intranet.

For Sale - Dictionary of International law
3rd edition, vgc. No longer needed.
Cost £35, sell for £10 ono.
Tel: 01763 246098 (eve only)

FOR SALE

Wanted - Japanese translator
To translate scientific paper.
Will pay £50.
Email Trisha: tr2456@ur.ac.uk

Turkish teacher wanted
Student wants basic
Turkish tuition.
Open to offers.
Contact Steve on
01763 249077

2 Why are these advertisements written as notes? Choose the best answer.
a People don't look at notice boards for long. They won't read long advertisements.
b There can be many advertisements on a notice board.
c The advertisements are on small cards. You can't write long sentences.

Did you know ...?

We often write advertisements on postcards. We shorten or abbreviate words (e.g. *ono, vgc, eve. only*) because we only have a small space to write in.

3 Find these abbreviations in the advertisements on the notice board. Write the full expressions.

ono = o r̲ n̲ e̲ a̲ r̲ e̲ s̲ t̲
o f̲ f̲ e̲ r̲
vgc = v _ _ _ g _ _ _
c _ _ _ _ _ _ _ _
eve. only = eve _ _ _ _ _ only

4 Check your answers to Exercise 3 by looking again at the advertisement *Law book for sale – bargain* on page 54.

Plan

5 Ian is selling a bicycle and wants to put a card on the notice board. He is rewriting an advertisement he wrote for the intranet. Think about how to turn his sentences into notes.

For sale – Man's road bike
It's got 10 gears. ª I bought it two months ago. It's in excellent condition. I'm selling it for £30 ᵇbecause I was given a new one for my birthday. Phone Ian on 079630257832 or 0763 245406 (daytime).

6 **Look at Exercises 4 and 5 on page 55. Use short expressions from these exercises to replace the longer <u>underlined</u> ones in Ian's advertisement in Exercise 5 on page 56.**

a ....

....

b ....

....

7 **Look at these sentences. What words can Ian cross out? Cross them out for him.**

a ~~It's got~~ 10 gears.

b It's in excellent condition.

c I'm selling it for £30.

8 **Look at your own intranet advertisement for the microwave or the car share. Think about how you can change it to an advertisement for a notice board.**

a <u>Underline</u> anything that you make shorter.

b Cross out any words that are unnecessary.

Write

9 **Rewrite your advertisement. Make it shorter by cutting out anything that is not necessary and turning your sentences into notes.**

E X tra practice

– Look at the advertisements that you wrote in *Extra Practice* on page 56. Rewrite one for a notice board.

– Use the **Check** questions above to check your advertisements.

– Ask your teacher or a native speaker to check that they understand your advertisements.

Check

– Does your advertisement give all the important information?

– Does your title explain what you want or what you are selling?

– Have you cut anything that is not important?

– Does the reader know who to contact?

– Does the reader know how to contact the advertiser?

– Have you written in notes?

Class bonus

This is a game that tests how well you know the other students in your class.

1 Work with another student. Think about what things the people in your class like. Choose one thing that most of your classmates would like to buy.

2 Pretend that you are selling that thing. Decide on a good price. Write an advert for the class notice board.

3 Swap your advert with another pair of students.

4 Use the **Check** questions to check the other pair's advert. If it is unclear, explain to the other pair what they need to correct in their advert.

4 Swap back and correct your own advert (if you need to correct it).

5 Your teacher will put all the class's adverts in different places around the room.

6 Read all the adverts. In your pair, choose the advert that describes the thing that you most want to buy.

7 When your teacher tells you to, stand next to the advert. The advert with most people standing next to it, wins!

Can-do checklist

Tick what you can do.

	Can do	Need more practice
I can write short advertisements for an intranet.	✓	✓
I can write short advertisements for a notice board.		
I can write sentences in note form.		

Unit 12
At the library

Get ready to *write*

Think about these questions:
- What do you think this book is about?
- Does it look interesting?
- Would you like to read it? Why or why not?
- Do you think a science student might read it? Why or why not?
- How do you choose a book to read?

go to Useful language p. 83

Book reviews

Look at an example

Book Review

Title ⟶ *Why does a ball bounce?*

Author ⟶ by Adam Hart-Davis

Publisher ⟶ Ebury Press

Fiction/non-fiction ⟶ Non-fiction

Adam Hart-Davis loves photography, science and explaining things. He believes everyone can enjoy science and writes in clear, informal English. In this book there are 101 of his beautiful photographs. Next to each picture he asks a simple question and then tries to answer it.

What is the book about? ⟶ Why is the sky blue? Why is a shower warmer in the middle? What's the
What is the most important idea? ⟶ oldest thing alive?

Mr Hart-Davis is not an expert. He had a lot of help from scientists and uses information from their studies and the history of science for his explanations.

Why does a ball bounce? is full of popular science. Serious scientists
What do you think about the book? ⟶ may find it a little boring but I think it is fascinating. I recommend it to everyone with an interest in the world around us.

Name of reviewer ⟶ Reviewer: Giulio Siliotti

1 Complete this rule with one of the words in brackets ( ).

Reviewers normally use .... tenses. (past/present)

58 *Work and Study*

2 Look at the review of *Why does a ball bounce?* Complete these facts about the book.

a	Title	Why does a ball bounce?
b	Author	
c	Publisher	
d	Fiction/Non-fiction	

3 Giulio, the writer of the review, answers these questions in his review.
What is the book about? What is the most important idea? The questions for fiction books are different. Rearrange the jumbled words below to make questions.

a What / story / of / is / type / it / ?
   What type of story is it?

b When / happen / the story / does / ?
   _____

c Where / happen / the story / does / ?
   _____

d Who / characters / ? / are / most important / the
   _____

e What / ? / happens
   _____

Did you know …?

- A person who writes a book is called an *author*.
- A company that makes books is called a *publisher*.
- A story book is called *fiction*.
- An information book is called *non-fiction*.
- A person in a book is called a *character*.
- The story in a *fiction* book can happen in more than one place, e.g. Istanbul and Vienna.

4 In the last paragraph of the review Giulio says what he thinks about the book. What does he write to show that he is giving an opinion and not stating a fact? Write the words he uses.

_____
_____

5 Choose from the expressions below to say what you think about *Why does a ball bounce?*

a This is a(n) awful / good / great book.
   This is a good book.

b I hate/like/love this book because … (*say why*)
   _____

c If you like … (*say what*), you'll like this.
   _____

6 Match these non-fiction books to their subjects.

a *Life with Picasso* by Françoise Gilot and Carlton Lake / *Evita, First Lady* by John Barnes
b *The Origins of Species* by Charles Darwin / *Why Don't Penguins Feet Freeze?* by Mick O'Hare
c *Building a Website for Dummies* by David A. Crowder / *The Google Story* by David A. Vise
d *1421: The Year China Discovered America* by Gavin Menzies / *Ancient Rome* by Simon Baker

History
Science
Biography
Computing

7 What type of stories are these fiction books?

a *Dreaming of you* by Lisa Kleypas / *Simply Love* by Mary Balogh
b *I, Robot* by Isaac Asimov / *The Hitchhiker's Guide to the Galaxy* by Douglas Adams
c *Helen of Troy* by Margaret George / *The Name of the Rose* by Umberto Eco
d *Death on the Nile* by Agatha Christie / *Looking Good Dead* by Peter James

Sci-fi
Detective / murder mystery / crime
Romance
Historical novel

Focus on ...
linking

| a sentence | and | a sentence |

Okay		Better
Adam Hart-Davis loves photography. He loves science.	→	Adam Hart-Davis loves photography and science.
Adam Hart-Davis loves photography and science and explaining things.	→	Adam Hart-Davis loves photography, science and explaining things.
He believes everyone can enjoy science and writes in clear and chatty English.	→	He believes everyone can enjoy science and writes in clear, chatty English.

1 Look at the examples and complete these suggestions about how to improve your linking. Use *and* or a comma?
   a Use .... to link two similar things in one sentence.
   b Use .... to link things in a list.
   c Use .... to link the two things at the end of a list.
   d Use .... to link adjectives that give similar information about a thing.

2 Are these statements correct ✓ or incorrect ✗?
   a He asks a simple question and then tries to answer it.
   b He has had a lot of help from scientists, he uses information from their studies.

3 Link these sentences. Use *and* or a comma.
   The Hound of the Baskervilles is a story about a curse. It's a story about a supernatural dog.

4 Complete each box with *and* or a comma.
   a It's set on dark [____] damp Dartmoor.
   b The main characters are Dr Watson [____] the American Sir Henry Baskerville [____] his neighbours.
   c Sir Henry takes Watson with him to Baskerville Hall [____] Holmes solves the mystery.

Plan

8 **Imagine that you are studying English Literature. You want to read a Sherlock Holmes story. Your friend has shown you this one that she borrowed from the library. Look at the book cover. What do you think it is about?**

PENGUIN CLASSICS

ARTHUR CONAN DOYLE
The Hound of the Baskervilles

Learning tip

We use commas and full stops to show where we pause when we speak.
- A full stop is a pause when you can take a breath. It shows an idea is complete.
- A comma is only a short pause. It shows an idea is not finished.

When you are checking your writing for commas and full stops read it out and see where you pause.

9 Giulio is writing a review of *The Hound of the Baskervilles*. Here are his notes. Help him by completing the facts about the book.

^aTitle:
^bAuthor:
^cFiction/Non-fiction

Type of story
- Sherlock Holmes
- detective story

Who?
- Holmes (sometimes)
- Dr Watson
- Sir Henry Baskerville (American)
- neighbours

When? Where?
- over 100 years ago
- London and Dartmoor → dark, damp

Good or bad?
- good for people who like crime fiction
- good for people who like mysteries

Write

10 **Complete the sentences below. You can use Guilio's notes, Exercises 2–8 on pages 59–60 and sentences from *Focus on linking* to write the review.**

The Hound of the Baskervilles is a .... story.
It's a story about ....
It's set ....
The main characters are ....
Sir Henry ....

This is a good book. I like it because you never know what's going to happen next. If you like .... , you'll like this.

Check

– Have you written the facts about the book?
– Have you answered all the questions in the flow chart?
– Have you written how good you think the book is?
– Will your review help other people to decide if they want to read the book?
– Have you put Giulio's name and your name at the bottom of the review?
– Have you checked that you have used commas and *and* correctly?

Class bonus

1 In small groups, write a list of five books that you have read or that are famous.
2 On you own, choose one book from the list. Do not tell the other students the name of the book.
3 Write a review. Do not write the book or author's name anywhere in the review.
4 Read the reviews that the other students have written. Guess which book each review is about.
5 At the end, as a group, decide on the top three books from your list (1 = most popular, 3 = least popular).

E tra practice

– Write a review of a book you have read.
– Ask an English-speaking friend or teacher to check it.
– Search for the book on www.Amazon.com
– Post your book review on Amazon.
– After two weeks, look at the review again. See how helpful people have found it.

Can-do checklist

Tick what you can do.

	Can do	Need more practice
I can write a book review.	✓	✓
I can link sentences using *and* and commas.	✓	✓

Unit 13
No time!

Get ready to *write*

Ravi Annaji

- What do you think Ravi's job is? Tick ✓ one box.
  a doctor ☐
  b salesperson ☐
  c teacher ☐
  d bank manager ☐

  ● 14) You are at home. You are not expecting a phone call. The phone rings. It's Ravi Annaji. Listen and check your answer.

- Look at these sentences. Are they true (T) or false (F)?
  a Ravi is selling insurance. ......
  b Ravi wants to meet you. ......

- When you get this type of phone call what do you normally do?
  Say you have no time and put the phone down. ☐
  Listen and then say you do not want to buy anything. ☐
  Reply in a rude way. ☐
  Make an appointment. ☐

go to Useful language p. 83

A Notes for important conversations

Look at an example

These are the notes Ravi wrote before his telephone call in *Get ready to write*.

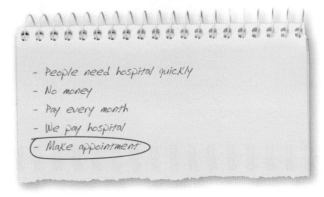

- People need hospital quickly
- No money
- Pay every month
- We pay hospital
- Make appointment

This is what Ravi says in the telephone call.

> People never think they'll get sick or have an accident. Then they need private hospital treatment quickly but don't have the money to pay for it. You don't want that to happen to you, do you? Well, our new Health Insurance plan can save you all the worry.
> You pay us some money every month and if you do need to go to hospital, we'll pay for it. Simple!
> Now, perhaps I could fix an appointment to see you. Then I could explain it all to you …

---

1 <u>Underline</u> the rules for notes.
   a Notes are long. / <u>Notes are short</u>.
   b Notes use complete sentences. / Notes use important words only.
   c Notes give all the information you know. / Notes only give important information.
   d Notes are easy to remember. / Notes are difficult to remember.

Plan

2 Ravi wants to ask his boss for more money. He is a good salesman. Look at the list of things he wants to tell his boss:

> 1 I work very hard.
> 2 I sell more insurance than anybody in the company.
> 3 I'm very polite and I'm never late.
> 4 All my workmates like me.

3 Which of these things is most important to his boss? Put them in the best order to tell him.

a ....
b ....
c ....
d ....

4 Make Ravi's notes easier to remember by crossing out unimportant words.

> 1 ~~I~~ work ~~very~~ hard.
> 2 I sell more insurance than anybody in the company.
> 3 I'm very polite and I'm never late.
> 4 All my workmates like me.

5 Silvia is a teacher. She has agreed to meet Ravi Annaji to find out more about the Health Insurance Plan. She wants to write some notes to help her remember what to ask Ravi. Help Sylvia write her notes.

Silvia Gonzalez

She thinks …	She wants to ask Ravi Annaji …	She writes …
It may be expensive.	How much does it cost?	a Cost?
Older people can't buy it.	Am I the right age?	b
Some hospitals are good. Some hospitals are bad.	Can I choose the hospital?	c

6 You want to buy a BMW car. The garage has only got one. Here are three questions to ask the car salesman. Write one more question.

a What colour is it?
b Is it new?
c Does the price include tax?
d ....

7 a Put the questions from Exercise 6 in the best order for you.

b Cross out unimportant words in the questions.

Write

8 Write notes to help you remember what you want to ask the car salesperson.

1
2
3
4

Check

– Are your notes in the best order?
– Are your notes easy to remember?
– Are your notes short?
– Have you used only important words?

E**X**tra practice

You want a new company car. What do you want to tell your boss? Write notes.

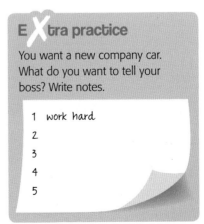

1 work hard
2
3
4
5

B Notes on appointments

Look at an example

1 Look at Silvia's diary. Are these statements true (T) or false (F)?

a The diary includes notes about things that are easy for Sylvia to remember. __F__

b It includes notes about new things. ......

c It includes things that change from week to week. ......

d It includes times she must do things. ......

e It is written in complete sentences. ......

30 monday

Basketball (after school)

31 tuesday

16.15 - New parents' meeting

1 wednesday

Basketball (after school)

thursday 2

Must correct books for Friday

friday 3

16.30 meeting with Principal

saturday 4

sunday 5

WEEK 31

Plan

2 Ravi Annaji only visits customers in the afternoon, from 14.00 to 17.00. He travels long distances and each visit takes one hour. This includes travelling time. How should Ravi organize his appointments to make best use of his time? Choose one answer.

a He should visit people who live near each other.

b He should only visit people who live in the city centre.

c He should visit people in the same order they phoned him (e.g. he should first visit the person who phoned him first.)

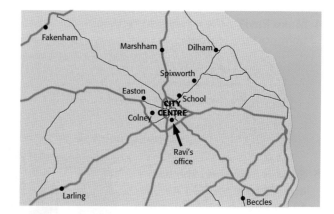

3 You are an Administrative Assistant at BL Insurance. You have to help the sales people organize their time. These are your notes about customers that Ravi could visit. Ravi only has time to visit four people. Look at the map and choose the best four people for him to visit.

Ms Partridge at Colney phoned about life insurance. Can you make an appointment?

Can you visit Mr Blair? He's at Beccles.

Mrs Betty from Fakenham needs car insurance.

Visit Julie Appleton at Easton.

Mr Polge (Spixworth) wants to make an appointment to talk about health insurance. Phone back!

Mr Davids (Dilham) rang. Wants to talk to you about house insurance.

4 You are going to add the four appointments to Ravi's personal organizer. Look at the notes for the people you chose in Exercise 3. Make the notes shorter by crossing out unimportant words. e.g.

Mr Davids (Dilham) ~~rang. Wants to talk to you about~~ house insurance.

Write

5 Add the four appointments to Ravi's personal organizer.

Monday
· ·
· ·
16.30 Ms Gonzalez, Norwich High School
Tuesday
· ·
· ·
16.00 - Meeting boss (more money!)

Focus on ...
spelling days and months

1 Use these letters to complete the days of the week. At the end there will be four letters left.

j ө ʀ u e s e d n e s e h u r s r i a t u r u n u n

a M o n day   e F _ _ day
b T _ _ _ day   f S _ _ _ _ day
c W _ _ _ _ _ day   g S _ _ day
d T _ _ _ _ day

2 The four letters that you have not used spell a month. What is it? _ _ _ _

3 Tick the months that are spelt correctly. Correct those that are not spelt correctly.
a Janury *January*   g July
b Febry   h Agust
c March   i September
d Aprill   j October
e May ✓   k November
f June   l Desember

Learning tip
Remember, days and months always have a capital letter.

Extra practice

Ravi is at a meeting. His boss is explaining about new car insurance that the company is going to sell.
- Listen to ●15. Write short notes to help Ravi remember the most important information.
- Now look at the audioscript ●15 on page 94. Cross out any words or information that are not important. e.g. ~~You can~~ start selling ~~our new~~ car insurance ~~on~~ Monday.
- Check if your notes and your shortened audioscript are the same.
- Complete Ravi's diary for the next week.

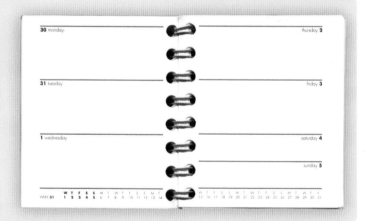

Can-do checklist
Tick what you can do.

	Can do	Need more practice
I can make short notes for my own use.	✓	✓
I can enter appointments in a diary or an electronic organizer.		

Unit 14
Out of the office

go to Useful language p. 84

Get ready to write

🔊 16 You are trying to contact Kenzo Asaki. Listen to the phone message. Why has he not answered the phone?

Having a really bad time.
Wish you were here!

Back on the 3rd!
Kenzo

You have 8 faxes, 257 emails and 53 voicemails.

Look at the pictures and think about these questions.
a Where is Kenzo? What is he doing? Is he having a good time?
b Where is Shona? Is she having a good time? Why or why not?

A Out of the office message

Look at an example

File Edit View Insert Format Tools Message Help

From: Kenzo@soloto.co.uk
Date: 21 April
Subject: Out of the Office auto-reply

¹ Thank you for your email message to Kenzo Asaki. I am away from the office from 19 April until 3 May.

² If you need to contact someone urgently, please phone Shona Stevens on 01438 325835 or email her at shona@soloto.co.uk

³ I will reply to your message as soon as I can when I come back.

---

1 Look at the email. Why did Peter receive this message? Tick ✓ one of the boxes.

a Kenzo is away. ☐
b Kenzo is busy. ☐
c Kenzo does not work for the company anymore. ☐

2 Look at the subject heading of the email. What do you think an auto-reply is? Tick ✓ one of the boxes.

a A message that you send when you come back to work. ☐
b A reply that a workmate sends when you are away. ☐
c A message that you send before you go away. ☐
d A reply that a computer sends when you are away. ☐

3 Where can you find the answers to these questions in the email? Write the numbers.

a   When is Kenzo away? ___1___
b   What will Kenzo do when he comes back? _____
c   What can you do if you need an immediate reply? _____

4 Match the sentences below to sentences in the email.

a   For urgent queries, please contact Shona Stevens.
    <u>If you need to contact someone urgently, please</u>
    <u>phone Shona Stevens.</u>

b   Unfortunately, I am not available until 3 May.

    ----

c   I will email you when I return.

Focus on ...
from + until, for

When are you on holiday?
I'm going on holiday from 19 April until / to 3 May.

  Start date   Finish date

How long are you going on holiday for?
I'm going to Spain for two weeks. (Period of time)

1   Complete these sentences.
    a   Nelson Mandela was in prison ..*from*.. 1962
        ..*until*.. 1990. He was in prison *for 28* years.
    b   The 2006 Winter Olympics ran _____ 10 February
        _____ 26 February. They ran _____ days.
    c   The Beatles sang together _____ 1960 _____
        1970. They were together _____ years.

2   Think about your last holiday. Write two sentences saying when you went away and how long you went away for.
    I _____ from
    _____ until
    _____ .
    I _____ for
    _____ .

Plan

5 Imagine you work in a company. Today is 22 November. Read this note from your boss, Lene Moller. Answer the questions.

At the Oslo office from tomorrow for two days. Pass on anything urgent to Marta Miranda (01438 325839).

Lene

a   When is Lene leaving?
    ----
b   When is Lene returning?
    ----
c   What should someone do if they have an urgent query?

Write

6 Lene wants you to set up auto-reply on his computer. Write the email that the computer will send while he is away.

Check

–   Have you written the date when Lene leaves?
–   Have you written when Lene will return?
–   Have you written what Lene will do when he arrives back?
–   Have you written what someone can do if they need an immediate reply?
–   Have you used *from*, *until* and *for* correctly?
–   Ask a native speaker or teacher to read the message and check that they understand it.

Extra practice

–   Think about your last holiday. Write an auto-reply message for your computer. (If you do not work, give your mobile number as the emergency contact number.)
–   Use the **Check** questions to check your message.

B A telephone message

Look at an example

1 (17) **Look at Shona's notes. Listen to the telephone conversation she had with the customer. Who does the customer want to talk to?**

> 2 May, 10.15
> Mrs Rosen
> Ordering more?
> Bigger discount?
> Phone back.
> 0206 788 9876

☎ **Telephone Message**

1
For:	Kenzo Asaki
From:	Mrs Rosen, IWS Ltd.
Taken by:	Shona Stevens
Date and time:	2 May, 10.15

2 Please call them. ✓   Will call back. ☐   Urgent. ✓

Message

3 Mrs Rosen phoned about possibly ordering more. Can you offer a bigger discount? I said that you'd phone back when you returned. Her number is 0206 788 9876.

2 **Look at the message Shona wrote from her notes. Put these questions in the order they are answered.**

a Who phoned?
b What did the writer say will happen next?
c What did they phone about?

    _a_   _____   _____

3 **Where are these things on the message form?**

a The message 3
b Details about the call, the caller and who took the message ☐
c What will happen next ☐

Focus on ...
words that people often misspell, mistype or get confused

Most people use a spell checker when they write using a computer. Sometimes computers get it wrong! Here is an email message that the spell checker thinks is correct.

> Mrs Rosen ordered 500 printer cartridges from the company last week. She wants to by more an says they shouldn't be to expensive. She also wants to talk about other thinks with you. Please phone her back.

1 a <u>Underline</u> four mistakes in the message.
  b Correct the mistakes.

2 Here are many words that people often misspell, mistype or get confused. Choose the correct word to complete the sentence.

a I went _____to_____ my mother's house.   (to/too/two)
b London is _____ crowded for me.   (to/too/two)
c I have _____ sisters.   (to/too/two)
d It's a story _____ Sir Arthur Conan Doyle.   (by/buy/bye)
e I want to _____ a new car.   (by/buy/bye)
f _____ ! See you soon.   (By/Buy/Bye)
g I can speak French _____ English.   (an/and)
h I don't _____ Maria's boss.   (know/no)
i Welcome to _____ school!   (or/our)
j _____ do you know in your new class?   (How/Who)
k Sue and Paul want to borrow our laptop.
  _____ computer's broken.   (Their/There)
l I've just got a letter _____ Grandma.   (form/from)

Learning tip

Write a word that you often confuse with another or misspell. _____
Every time you write something, remember to check your spelling of that word.

Plan

4 🔊 **18 Listen to another telephone conversation and (circle) the answers.**

a   Who is the message for?   Shona   Kenzo   Marta
b   Who is the message from?   Shona   Kenzo   Marta
c   What is the message about?   a meeting   an email   Kenzo's holiday

5   Complete this part of the message form.

☎ **Telephone Message**

For: _____
From: _____
Taken by: _____

6   Look at the notes Shona made.

2 May, 12.15
Marta Miranda
Meeting on Wednesday.
Friday?
She'll phone back or email.

7   Use the notes to help you choose which box to tick.

Please call them ☐   Will call back ☐   Urgent ☐

8   Now answer Kenzo's questions.

a   Who phoned? ....
b   What did she ask? ....
c   Should I phone her back? ....

Write

9   Write the message to Kenzo.

Message _____
_____
_____
_____

Check

– Does the reader know who phoned?
– Does the reader know what the person wanted?
– Does the reader know what should happen next?
– Does the reader know when the message was taken?
– Does the reader know who took the message?
– Have you checked any words that you often misspell, mistype or get confused?

Class bonus

1   Student A: Imagine you work for a company that does business with Soloto. Think of a problem you might have, e.g. Soloto didn't send the things you ordered. Phone Kenzo Asaki about your problem.
Student B: You work for Soloto. Kenzo is out of the office at the moment. Answer the phone and take a message. Start by saying: *Hello, Soloto. How can I help you?*

2   With your partner, check to see if you have written the correct message.
3   Now swap roles: Student B phone Kenzo and Student A write the message.

Can-do checklist

Tick what you can do.

	Can do	Need more practice
I can write an auto-reply message.		
I can write telephone messages.		
I can use *from*, *until* and *for* correctly.		
I can correct common spelling errors.		

Unit 15

Can you help me?

Get ready to write

Enter password

******

Incorrect password. Try again

○ Pete Banks is a salesperson for a company that sells electronic equipment. He is at home. He is trying to log on to his company's computer system. Think about these questions.

a What is the problem?

b Have you had a similar problem?

c What did you do about it?

go to Useful language p. 84

An informal request

Look at an example

1 Look at the email Pete sent to Anne. Why did he send it? Tick ✓ one of the boxes.

a Pete is worried that Anne doesn't like him. He wants to explain that he is not stupid. ☐

b Pete wants Anne to tell people that he will not be in the office tomorrow. ☐

c Pete has forgotten his password. He wants Anne to email the password to him. ☐

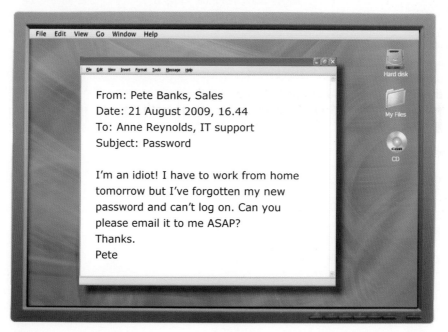

File Edit View Go Window Help

File Edit View Insert Format Tools Message Help

From: Pete Banks, Sales
Date: 21 August 2009, 16.44
To: Anne Reynolds, IT support
Subject: Password

I'm an idiot! I have to work from home tomorrow but I've forgotten my new password and can't log on. Can you please email it to me ASAP?
Thanks.
Pete

2 This memo is from the company's Managing Director, Fabiana Lopez. Why did she send it to all the people in the Sales Department? Tick ✓ one of the boxes.

a Fabiana wants someone from the Sales Department to phone Julian Mann. ☐

b Fabiana wants everyone to know that Julian Mann has a problem with the company. She wants the Sales Department to be nice to him when he phones. ☐

c Fabiana wants someone from the Sales Department to return MP3 players to Julian Mann. ☐

MEMO

To: Sales Department
From: Fabiana Lopez
Date: 21 August 2009

Subject: ICWG

Julian Mann from ICWG phoned me yesterday. He is worried about the quality of the MP3 players we are selling them. He says they returned 30% of the last order because they didn't work. He may phone one of you. Please, be nice to him. We don't want to lose his business!

Plan

3 a Look at these ways of *asking* people to do something.

Asking people to do things: Yes/no questions	More polite
Can you help me?	Can you help me please?
Can I have …?	Can I have …, please?

b Who can you *ask* to do something? Underline your answers.

a friend / your mother / your boss / a workmate / someone who works for you.

c Look at the email. Pete is not Anne's boss. He cannot *tell* her to do something. What does he *ask* her to do? Write Pete's question.

Can _____

4 a Look at these ways of *telling* people to do something.

Telling people to do things: statements	More polite
Do something for me.	Please do something.

b Who can you *tell* to do something? Underline your answers.

a friend / your mother / your boss / a workmate / someone who works for you.

c Look at the memo. Fabiana Lopez is Managing Director so she can *tell* the people in the Sales Department to do something. What does she *tell* them to do? Write Fabiana's statement.

Please _____

5 Make these statements more polite.

a Send 50 brochures to our Korean office.
Please send 50 brochures to our Korean office.

b Telephone Julian Mann.
_____

c Get someone to repair the photocopier.
_____

d Reply to this email as soon as you get it.
_____

Did you know …?

A memo (or memorandum) is a note from one person to another person (or other people) in the same company. A memo is written on a piece of paper. It is not sent electronically like an email.

A brochure is a book or pamphlet that contains information about the things that a company sells. Sometimes companies print a separate price list. They do this so that they can change their prices without printing new brochures.

6 Who are you most polite to? Put these in order: 1 (most polite) to 5 (least polite).

a a friend
b your mother
c your boss
d a workmate
e someone who works for you

71

7 You want people to do things for you. Decide if you will *ask* or *tell* them and how polite you will be. Then write your requests.

a You want a friend to reserve a table in *La Trattoria* restaurant for tonight.
Can you reserve a table at La Trattoria for tonight, please?

b You want your mother to get some cinema tickets for you.
----

c You want your boss to give you a pay rise.
----

d You want a workmate to email the price of the new MP3 players.
----

e You want someone who works for you to order more photocopier paper.

> **Learning tip**
>
> We use punctuation to show how we would say something if we were talking. Exclamation marks (!) show where you have written something exciting. When you read your writing check that you have not made everything sound too exciting. If you have, delete some exclamation marks.

Focus on ...

full stops (.), question marks (?) and exclamation marks (!)

Can you help me?   I need twenty brochures, please.
This is urgent!

1 Look at the examples above. Match the punctuation marks to the explanations.
   a This shows where a statement ends. —   **!**
   b This makes a statement stronger or shows that something is surprising or exciting.
   c This shows that you are asking something.   **.**
                                                          ?

2 Is this statement true (T) or false (F)?
   ? and ! go at the end of the sentence. ......

3 Complete these sentences. Use !, ? or .
   a That's wonderful
   b Thank you for your help
   c How many have you got

4 Sarah is helping to write a new brochure for the leisure centre. She is excited about what people can do there.

   The facilities at the leisure centre are amazing! There is a swimming pool, a gym and a multi-sports hall! There is also a sauna! Join and enjoy all these facilities free!

   a She has used too many exclamation marks. Underline three exclamation marks that can be changed to full stops.
   b Write the message correctly using exclamation marks and full stops.

Write

For paper and ink
contact Sandy Sharp

Printer

A4 paper

8 Look at the pictures. Imagine you work in this office. Answer these questions.

a Who do you need to send an email to?
Sandy Sharp

b What is the subject of the email?
----

c What do you want someone to do?
----

d Who do you want to do it?
----

e When do you want them to do it?
----

9 Write the email.

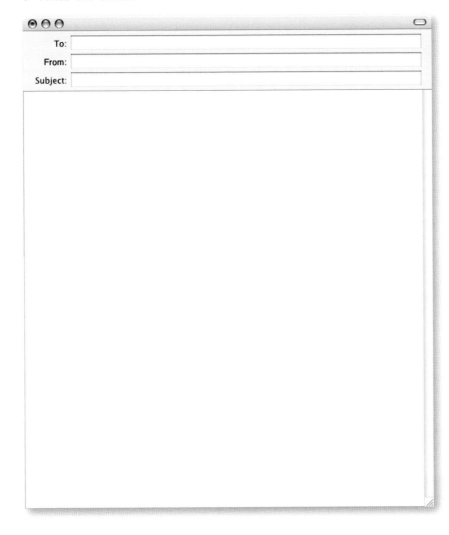

Check

- Think about the reader. Is it correct to *ask* or *tell* them to do something?
- Have you written what you want them to do?
- Have you written who you want to do it?
- Have you written when you want them to do it?
- Is your subject heading short?
- Does your subject heading give an idea of what the email is about?
- Have you used full stops, question marks and exclamation marks correctly?

E**X**tra practice

- Think about your workplace or school. Does anyone send memos or email requests?
- What are the memos or email requests about? E.g. change of rooms, extra lessons etc.
- Write a typical memo or email request for your workplace or school.
- Use the **Check** questions to correct your email.
- Ask your teacher or a native speaker to check your email.

Can-do checklist

Tick what you can do.

I can write friendly and informal emails and memo requests.

I can use *yes/no* questions and statements correctly when asking for things to be done.

I can use full stops, question marks and exclamation marks.

Can do	Need more practice

Unit 16
I would be grateful if ...

Get ready to write

From:	Li Xiao-Hong, Managing director, Paperless Publishing plc
Date:	25 June 2010, 10.18
To:	Sara Parsons, Resource Manager, Paperless Publishing plc
Subject:	Rain coming in!

The roof's leaking in the accounts department! Please get Surebuild to fix it ASAP. You'll need to email Clive Allen there.
Thanks.
Li

PS Please send me a copy of your email.

○ Look at the picture and the email. Think about these questions.
  a What's the problem?
  b What does Xiao-Hong Li want Sara Parsons to do about it?
  c How well does Xiao-Hong Li know Sara Parsons? How do you know?

go to Useful language p. 84

A formal request

Look at an example

1 Look at Sara's email. Why has Sara emailed Mr Allen? Tick ✓ one of the boxes.

a Sara's boss told her to email Mr Allen. ☐
b Mr Allen is a friend of hers. ☐
c She knows that Mr Allen works for Surebuild (UK) Ltd and that he is a good builder. ☐

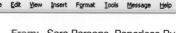

From:	Sara Parsons, Paperless Publishing plc
Date:	25 June 2010, 10.30
To:	Clive Allen, Surebuild (UK) Ltd.
Cc:	Li Xiao-Hong, Managing director, Paperless Publishing plc
Subject:	Urgent building work

Dear Mr Allen,

I would be grateful if you could arrange a time to come and look at our flat roof. It has suddenly started to leak badly.

I am sure you will appreciate that this is urgent as we do not want any of our electrical equipment to get wet.

Please email me to arrange a convenient time or contact me on my direct line, 01604 589345.

Thank you for your help.

Best regards
Sara Parsons, Resource Manager
Paperless Publishing plc

2 What does Sara want Mr Allen to do? Tick ✓ one of the boxes.

a She wants him to look at the electrical equipment and fix it. ☐
b She wants him to look at the flat roof and fix it. ☐
c She wants him to phone Li Xiao-Hong. ☐

3 Find words or expressions in Sara's email that have a similar meaning and write them below.

a Please
    I would be grateful if
b ASAP

c You'll

d Thanks

e Phone me

4 Are these rules for more polite and formal emails true (T) or false (F)?

a Use a closing expression (e.g. *Best regards*) and your name ..T..
b It is not necessary to use an opening expression but many people do, e.g. *Dear Mr Allen* ......
c Use abbreviations, e.g. *ASAP* ......
d Do not use contractions (e.g. *You'll*), use full forms (e.g. You will) ......
e Do not use PS ......

Learning tip

When you write letters or emails always ask yourself these questions:
How well do I know this person?
Can I write an informal and friendly email to them?
Do I need to write a more polite and formal email to them?
Use Appendix 7 on page 92 to help you write your email.

Plan

i Can you send me some information?
ii Could/Would you send me some information?
iii I would be grateful if you could send me some information.

FRIENDLY and INFORMAL
↓
MORE POLITE and FORMAL

5 Look at the examples above.

a Which request can you write to a workmate who you are friendly with? .....i.....
b Which request can you write to a workmate you have never met? ....
c Which request can you write to someone in another company? ....

6 Look carefully at iii. Think about how it is different to i and ii.

7 You are writing to a workmate who you are friendly with. Ask for some envelopes.

.... *send me some envelopes?*

8 You are writing to a workmate who you have never met. Ask for her ideas about the company's new product.

.... *tell me what you think about the company's new product?*

9 Write to someone in another company. Ask to arrange a meeting.

.... *arrange a meeting.*

10 Match these friendly and informal expressions with more polite and formal ones.

a Can we meet up?
b How about 25 June?
c I want to talk about your products.
d I want to ask when your office is open.
e Please send some brochures.
f Let me know what you think.
g See you soon.

1 I look forward to seeing you.
2 Please forward some brochures.
3 Would you be free on 25 June?
4 I look forward to hearing from you.
5 I would like to discuss your products.
6 Could we arrange a meeting?
7 I have an enquiry about your opening times.

Did you know ...?

Friendly and informal emails:
Begin a friendly and informal email with the person's first name (or no name at all). End the email with *Best wishes*.

More polite and formal emails:

US
Dear Ms Chi / Sincerely yours
Dear Sirs / Yours truly

UK
Dear Ms Chi / Yours sincerely
Dear Sirs / Yours truly
Dear Sir or Madam / Yours faithfully

Regards or *Best regards* can be used in the UK and US to end a more polite and formal email.

See Appendix 7 on page 92 for more examples of more polite and formal expressions.

Focus on ...
I, you, she, he, it, they

From: Sara Parsons, Paperless Publishing plc
Date: 25 June 2010, 10.30
To: Clive Allen, Surebuild (UK) Ltd.
Cc: Li Xiao-Hong, Managing director, Paperless Publishing plc
Subject: Urgent building work

Dear Mr Allen

I would be grateful if you could arrange a time to come and look at our flat roof. It has suddenly started to leak badly.

---

1 Link the pronouns in blue to the thing or person that they describe.

2 Complete this rule: Use a pronoun to refer to a .... or .... that you have already mentioned.

3 Use pronouns to replace the underlined words.
   Earlier this year, Mrs Ghumman forwarded some of your summer brochures to me. In her letter <u>Mrs Ghumman</u> said she would be happy to send more. <u>The brochures</u> have been very popular with our customers and we have given all of them away. Please could you send an extra 20?

4 Sometimes pronouns can confuse the reader. Look at the underlined pronouns below. Is it easy to understand who the person is or what the thing is? Write (u/c) next to unclear sentences.
   a Mrs Ghumman and Ms Patel work for a travel company. <u>She</u> is a sales representative. u/c
   b Mr Gibson will contact you shortly. <u>He</u> works in our customer relations department.
   c The TEXT2100 is a new product from our company. <u>It</u> has many successful products.
   d The TEXT2100 is a new pen-sized translator. You scan and <u>it</u> translates!

5 Correct the unclear sentences in 4. Use the name of the person or thing to make the sentences easier to understand.

Write

11 **Jo Grant has just started work at Paperless Publishing plc. She found this note on her desk. What does Li want her to do?**

----

12 This is the email Jo wrote. She has asked you to check it for her. What is wrong with it?

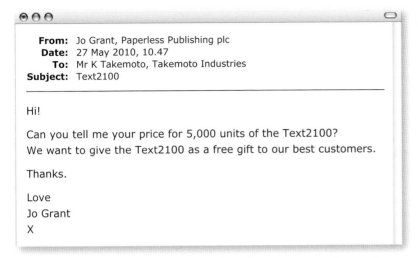

From: Jo Grant, Paperless Publishing plc
Date: 27 May 2010, 10.47
To: Mr K Takemoto, Takemoto Industries
Subject: Text2100

Hi!

Can you tell me your price for 5,000 units of the Text2100?
We want to give the Text2100 as a free gift to our best customers.

Thanks.

Love
Jo Grant
X

13 Help Jo by rewriting the email. Make it more polite and formal.

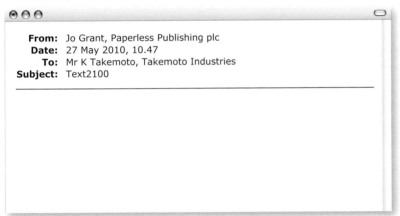

From: Jo Grant, Paperless Publishing plc
Date: 27 May 2010, 10.47
To: Mr K Takemoto, Takemoto Industries
Subject: Text2100

Check

- Can the reader understand what you want?
- Is your email more polite and formal?
- Have you used *could*, not *can*? Have you used *would* not *will*?
- Have you checked that the pronouns make the email easy to understand?
- Have you used appropriate expressions to begin and end the email?
- Have you made sure that you have not used abbreviations or contractions?

Can-do checklist

Tick what you can do.

	Can do	Need more practice
I can write more polite and formal email requests.		
I can use *could* and *would* appropriately.		
I can begin and end formal email requests.		

Review 2
Work and study

A Planning your writing

Choosing what to write

1 You answer the phone at work. The caller wants to speak to a workmate who is not there. What do you write to your workmate?

a notes   b a message   c an email or letter
d an advertisement

Knowing the reader

2 You are writing a telephone message to a colleague you have not met. What style will you use? Choose one:

a friendly and informal   b more polite and formal

3 You are writing an email to a colleague who you know well. What style will you use? Choose one:

a friendly and informal   b more polite and formal

4 You are writing notes on your timetable. Which of these things do you not include?

a teacher's name   b room number   c type of lesson
d your reason for taking that lesson

5 Which of these is the most important information to include in a book review?

a what you thought about the book
b when the book was published
c if the book is fiction or non-fiction
d the name of the publisher

B Checking your writing

Checking that the reader has enough information

6 Read this advertisement. What information is missing that the reader needs to know?

a what Tom wants   b the price Tom will pay
c Tom's contact details   d the condition

> ### Books needed
>
> I want American Literature books.
> Their condition is not too important.
> I will pay £20. Phone Tom.

7 Read this out of the office message. What information is missing that the reader needs to know?

From:	birgit@soloto.co.uk
Date:	15 June
To:	
Subject:	Out of the Office auto-reply

Thank you for your email message to Birgit Liden. I am away from the office. If you need to contact someone urgently, please phone Shona Stevens on 01438 325835. I will reply to your message as soon as I can.

a who to contact   b why Birgit cannot reply
c what Birgit will do next   d when Birgit will return

8 Read this telephone message.
What information could be cut?

> ᵃKenzo Asaki from Soloto phoned today at 15.30.
> ᵇHe said that you phoned yesterday while he was out of the office. ᶜHe was on holiday. ᵈCan you phone him? He is happy to talk about the level of discount.

Checking that the information is well organized

9 Decide which <u>underlined</u> pronoun is confusing and should be replaced with a name.

a Chinua Achebe wrote *Things Fall Apart*. <u>He</u> comes from Nigeria.

b Adhaf Soueif is a woman writer. <u>She</u> is an Egyptian.

c Thomas Keneally writes about Jimmie Blacksmith in this book. <u>He</u> is a native Australian.

d Steve Irwin was called the Crocodile hunter. <u>He</u> wrote this book with his wife.

10 Some of the chairs in your office are broken and dangerous. Your boss does not like spending money, but you want him to buy new chairs. You make some notes about chairs to buy. Which set of notes is in the best order?

a
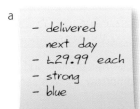
- delivered next day
- £29.99 each
- strong
- blue

b
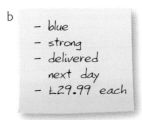
- blue
- strong
- delivered next day
- £29.99 each

c
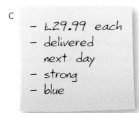
- £29.99 each
- delivered next day
- strong
- blue

d

- strong
- blue
- delivered next day
- £29.99 each

11 Look at the use of commas and *and* in these sentences. Which is best organized?

a Could you please advise me of the colours the price?

b Could you please advise me of the colour, price and delivery date for the chairs?

c Could you please advise me of the colour and price and delivery date for the chairs?

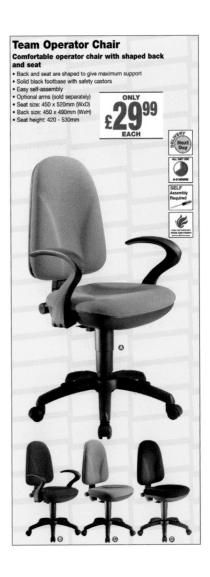

Team Operator Chair
Comfortable operator chair with shaped back and seat
- Back and seat are shaped to give maximum support
- Solid black footbase with safety castors
- Easy self-assembly
- Optional arms (sold separately)
- Seat size: 450 x 520mm (WxD)
- Back size: 450 x 490mm (WxH)
- Seat height: 420 - 530mm

ONLY
£29⁹⁹
EACH

Checking style

12 Here are four ways of saying the same thing. Which is best for an out of the office auto-reply message?

a Am on holiday. Shan't be back for a week. Cool! Leave a message with Vicky on 01376 998792

b I'm not here. Talk to Vicky on 01376 998792

c I am away from the office until 16 November. For urgent queries please contact Victoria Limbach on 01376 998792

13 Which of these would you write in a more polite and formal email or letter to someone you do not know?

a PS b Hi
c Yours sincerely d Love

14 You are in the UK. You are writing to a company. You do not know the name of the person you are writing to. How do you begin and end your letter?

a Dear Sir, / Sincerely yours,
b Dear Sir / Yours sincerely
c Dear Sir or Madam / Yours faithfully
d Dear Mr or Mrs, / Yours truly,

15 What would you write in an email to a senior manager who you do not know?

a Give me a holiday.
b Please give me a holiday.
c Can I have a holiday, please?
d I would be grateful if I could have a holiday.

Checking punctuation

16 Which of these emails has the best punctuation?

a

From:	Sarah Parsons
Date:	20 June 2010
To:	Photocopier services
Subject:	Help!

Can you help us, please? The photocopier has broken and we need to copy 1,000 letters before tomorrow. Please send someone immediately.

b

From:	Sarah Parsons
Date:	20 June 2010
To:	Photocopier services
Subject:	Help!

Can you help us, please? The photocopier has broken and we need to copy 1,000 letters before tomorrow. Please send someone immediately?

c

From:	Sarah Parsons
Date:	20 June 2010
To:	Photocopier services
Subject:	Help!

Can you help us, please. The photocopier has broken and we need to copy 1,000 letters before tomorrow. Please send someone immediately.

d

From:	Sarah Parsons
Date:	20 June 2010
To:	Photocopier services
Subject:	Help!

Can you help us, please? The photocopier has broken and we need to copy 1,000 letters before tomorrow! Please send someone immediately!

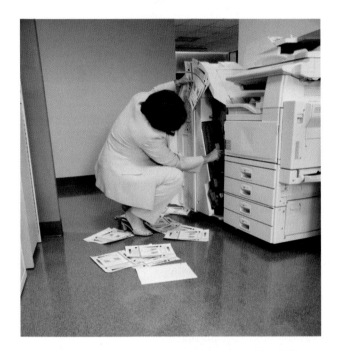

17 Where is the best place to replace the full stop with an exclamation mark?

Nelson Mandela's biography is amazing [a]. It tells his whole story and that of the ANC [b]. It explains how he lived in prison and how he forgave his enemies [c]. I recommend it to anyone who is interested in people [d].

18 Which of these is correct?

a Please send a brochure?
b Can you send a brochure, please?
c I would be grateful if you could send a brochure?
d Send a brochure?

Checking grammar

19 Look at the pronouns (he, she it, they). Which is incorrect?

a Mrs Ghumman works in our Paris office. She is a sales representative.
b I want to sell some books. It's in very good condition.
c I hope you like the new chairs. They were very cheap!
d Mr Patak will phone you back. He's on holiday at the moment.

20 Look at the prepositions (from, until, for). Which of these is incorrect?

a The college year runs from September until July.
b Each term or semester lasts for 12 weeks.
c Lectures run from 9.00 on most mornings.
d Some classes last until one hour.

Checking vocabulary

21 You are writing an advertisement. Which of these describes the condition of the thing you are selling?

a ono
b vgc
c eve. only
d Will pay £50

Checking spelling

22 Which word is spelt correctly?

a advertisement b avertisment c advertisment
d advetisement

23 Which word is spelt incorrectly?

a January b Februry c March d April

24 Which word is spelt incorrectly?

a Munday b Tuesday c Wednesday d Thursday

25 Which of these is correct?

a I want to bye a French grammar book.
b The chairs were expensive to by.
c I want to order two chairs.
d I want too order two chairs.

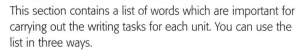

Appendix 1
Useful language

This section contains a list of words which are important for carrying out the writing tasks for each unit. You can use the list in three ways.

1 You can look at the list before you begin the unit and make sure that you understand the meaning of the words by looking them up in a dictionary.
2 You can look at the list before you begin the unit, but try to work out the meaning of the words when you see them in the unit.
3 You can look at the list when you have completed the unit and check that you understand the words.

When you start using the book, you may prefer to use the list in the first way. However, you will find each word in one of the texts, and the context – the words around the new word – will help you to work out its meaning. As you develop your writing skills, you will probably find that you do not have to look at the list before you begin the unit. You may already know some of the words; others you will be able to work out from the text or the task.

Each list is a record of the important vocabulary of the unit. You can use it as a checklist when you have completed the unit. There is space after each word to write a translation in your own language or an English expression using the word. Mark each word that you understand and can use with a highlighter pen.

There is also space below the wordlist for you to write other words from the units which are important to you. Look at Appendix 3 for ideas on what to record for each word.

Unit 1

en suite *adjective* _____
guest house *noun* _____
guest *noun* _____
arrival *noun* _____
departure *noun* _____
receptionist *noun* _____
hotel *noun* _____

Unit 2

customs *noun* _____
sender *noun* _____
parcel *noun* _____
send/receive something *verb* _____
sign for something *verb* _____
proof *noun* _____
value *noun* _____
valuable *adjective* _____

Unit 3

bank account *noun* _____
credit card *noun* _____
rent *noun* _____
mortgage *noun* _____
financial *adjective* _____
retired *adjective* _____
unemployed *adjective* _____
employment *noun* _____
residential *adjective* _____
current ≠ previous *adjectives* _____
employer *noun* _____
full-time *adjective* _____
part-time *adjective* _____
self-employed *adjective* _____
savings *noun* _____

Unit 4

hobby *noun* _____
nursing *noun* _____
leisure centre *noun* _____
international exchange programme *noun* _____
suburb *noun* _____
host *noun* _____
job *noun* _____
(university) course *noun* _____

Unit 5

message *noun* ....
(swimming) pool *noun* ....
pick someone up = collect someone *expression* ....
....
invite someone to do something *expression* ....
calendar *noun* ....
include *verb* ....
leisure centre *noun* ....
dentist *noun* ....
appointment *noun* ....

Unit 6

special occasions / events *nouns* ....
wedding *noun* ....
get married *expression* ....
anniversary *noun* ....
recovery *noun* ....
tasty *adjective* ....
gorgeous *adjective* ....
colourful *adjective* ....
fun *adjective* ....
unusual *adjective* ....
useful *adjective* ....
enjoyable *adjective* ....
interesting *adjective* ....
trendy *adjective* ....
great *adjective* ....
lovely *adjective* ....

Unit 7

celebration *noun* ....
invitation *noun* ....
wedding *noun* ....
event *noun* ....
arrangement *noun* ....
directions *noun* ....
accept *verb* ....
decline *verb* ....

Unit 8

ferry *noun* ....
scenery *noun* ....
festival *noun* ....
traditional *adjective* ....
fair *noun* ....
unnecessary *adjective* ....
view *noun* ....
bazaar *noun* ....
exotic *noun* ....
window shopping *noun* ....
temple *noun* ....
excursion *noun* ....
massive *adjective* ....

Unit 9

brilliant *adjective* ....
pass something to someone *expression* ....
....
paragraph *noun* ....
mark something *verb* ....
drop in on someone *expression* ....
touristy *adjective* ....

Unit 10

Director of studies *noun* ....
Social organizer *noun* ....
Accommodation officer *noun* ....
tutor *noun* ....
lecture *noun* ....
lecturer *noun* ....
list *noun* ....
essay *noun* ....
context *noun* ....
communicate *verb* ....
environment *noun* ....
global warming *noun* ....
warning *noun* ....
famous *adjective* ....
research something *verb* ....

Unit 11

second-hand *adjective* _____
advertisement *noun* _____
tuition *noun* _____
intranet *noun* _____
advertise *verb* _____
bargain *noun* _____
very good condition (vgc) *expression* _____
contact someone *expression* _____
negotiate a price *expression* _____
or nearest offer (ono) *expression* _____
hardly used *expression* _____
repair *noun* _____
duplicate *noun* _____
car-share *noun* _____
exchange *noun* _____
sale *noun* _____

Unit 12

author *noun* _____
title *noun* _____
subject *noun* _____
fiction *noun* _____
non-fiction *noun* _____
publisher *noun* _____
reviewer *noun* _____
fascinating *adjective* _____
popular *adjective* _____
opinion *noun* _____
evidence *noun* _____
curse *noun* _____
dark *adjective* _____
damp *adjective* _____
mystery *noun* _____
solve *verb* _____
supernatural *adjective* _____

Unit 13

salesperson *noun* _____
insurance *noun* _____
appointment *noun* _____
treatment *noun* _____
boss *noun* _____
customer *noun* _____
workmate *noun* _____
administrative assistant *noun* _____
company car *noun* _____

Unit 14

auto-reply *noun* _____
be away *expression* _____
workmate *noun* _____
queries (plural) *noun* _____
contact someone *expression* _____
urgently *adverb* _____
urgent *adjective* _____
pass on a message *expression* _____
make an arrangement *expression* _____
offer a discount *expression* _____

Unit 15

to log on *verb* _____
computer system *adjective + noun* _____
password *noun* _____
statement *noun* _____
memo *noun* _____
brochure *noun* _____
pamphlet *noun* _____
price list *adjective + noun* _____
pay rise *noun* _____

Unit 16

leak *noun* _____
leak *verb* _____
urgent *adjective* _____
fix something *expression* _____
convenient *adjective* _____
contraction *noun* _____
direct line *noun* _____
electrical equipment *noun* _____
product *noun* _____
building work *noun* _____
translator *noun* _____
unit *noun* _____

Appendix 2
What can I improve?

What do I want to do?

Do I want to ...?		Go to Unit ...
complete personal forms?	→	1, 2, 3
write personal email and letters?	→	4, 6, 9
leave messages?	→	5, 14
write cards for celebrations?	→	6
write thank you letters and email?	→	6
write an invitation?	→	7
accept or decline an invitation?	→	7
write a postcard?	→	8
make notes?	→	10, 13
write a short advertisement?	→	11
write a book review?	→	12
write a business email?	→	15, 16
write a friendly, informal request?	→	15
write a more polite and formal request?	→	16

How good is my writing?

Can I ...	No / Not sure		How important is this to me? (1= very important)		Go to Unit ...
write words when people spell them?		→		→	1, 10
write dates accurately?		→		→	1
use capital letters?		→		→	1
write addresses correctly?		→		→	2
write weights correctly?		→		→	2
write email addresses when people say them?		→		→	3
write a description of my family and hobbies?		→		→	4
write the titles and names of people correctly in emails and letters?		→		→	4
use sentences correctly?		→		→	4
write about sad and happy events?		→		→	6
use *because* to explain reasons?		→		→	7
write directions?		→		→	7
write about arrangements?		→		→	7
express opinions?		→		→	8, 12
make bad things sound better than they are?		→		→	8
address envelopes correctly?		→		→	9

Can I ...	No / Not sure		How important is this to me? (1= very important)		Go to Unit ...
use paragraphs correctly?		→		→	9
write sentences in note form?		→		→	11
link sentences using *and* and commas?		→		→	12
spell days of the week and months?		→		→	13
use *from, until* and *for* correctly?		→		→	14
correct words that I often misspell, mistype or get confused?		→		→	14
use *yes/no* questions and statements correctly when asking for things to be done?		→		→	15
use full stops, question marks and exclamation marks?		→		→	15
use *could* and *would* appropriately?		→		→	16
begin and end more polite and formal emails and letters?		→		→	16
plan and check my writing?		→		→	Appendix 3
think about my most frequent mistakes?		→		→	Appendix 4
talk about writing in English?		→		→	Appendix 5
understand English abbreviations?		→		→	Appendix 6
use more polite and formal English?		→		→	Appendix 7

Appendix 3
Check your writing

Planning

Think about these questions when you are writing.

Why am I writing?
Who is the reader going to be?
What am I writing about?
What information does the reader need?
What does the reader know about this subject already?
What type of writing should I use?

Checking questions

Use these questions to check your writing.

Communication
Does the reader understand why I am writing to them?

Information
Have I included all the information that the reader needs?
Have I cut any information that is not useful for the reader?
Have I repeated any information?

Organization
Have I organized my ideas and information logically?
Have I linked sentences together?
Is it easy to understand what the pronouns refer to?

Layout and style
Is this a letter? Have I put everything in the right place on the page?
Have I put the information into paragraphs? Have I put spaces between the paragraphs?
Is the writing personal, friendly and informal or more polite and formal? Is this correct for this reader?

Punctuation
Does the punctuation make the writing easy to understand?
Have I used a comma when I need a full stop?
Have I used an exclamation mark when I need a full stop?

Grammar
Have I used the right verb form?
Do the subject and verb agree in each sentence? Is the subject missing?
Are the words in the right order?
Have I used the right prepositions?
Have I checked the nouns? Are they uncountable? Are they plural?
Have I used the right article?

Capital letters
Have I used capital letters in the right place?

Vocabulary
Have I used the right word?
Can I use a specific word not a general one?
Is the word too weak or too strong?

Spelling
Have I checked that difficult words are spelt correctly?
Have I checked words that I often get wrong? e.g. to / two / too
If I am using a spell checker, have I also checked for meaning?
Have I used a dictionary to check words that I am not certain of?

Handwriting
Is my handwriting easy to understand?
Have I used capital letters and small letters?
Have I left enough space between words?
Have I left enough space after punctuation?
Have I left enough space between paragraphs?

Appendix 4
Check your mistakes

Write examples of the most frequent mistakes that you make in your writing here. Write the corrections too. Use this to check any writing you do in future.

Organization	
Layout	
Punctuation	
Grammar	
Capital letters	
Vocabulary	
Spelling	
Handwriting	

Appendix 5
Talk about your writing

These words and expressions will help you talk about your writing. Look them up in a dictionary and write an example. Write a definition for them in your own language.

	Example	Definition / Use
A question mark **?**	Can you help me please?	A question mark is a written or printed sign (?) that is put at the end of an expression or sentence to show that it is a question.
A comma **,**		
A full stop **.**		
An exclamation mark **!**		
A sentence		
A paragraph		
informal language		
formal language		
a letter		
a note		
a message		
to edit a piece of writing		
to delete something		

Add more abbreviations to the list as you find them. Write a definition for them in your own language.

Abbreviations	Example	Definition / Use
e.g.	We can print t-shirts in many exciting colours, *e.g.* blue, green, yellow, etc.	Here is an example or some examples (used before an example or some examples).
etc.	We can print t-shirts in many exciting colours, e.g. blue, green, yellow, *etc*.	And more similar things (used at the end of a list of things).
i.e.	There are two main different types of computers, *i.e.* PCs and Macs.	Here is an explanation (used before an explanation).
NB	*NB* Do not turn off the computer.	This is very important information (used at the beginning of a statement).
PS	*PS* Did I tell you that my sister's had a baby? He's lovely.	This is extra information (used before statements and questions at the end of a personal letter/email).
DoB	Date of birth 12/09/90	Date of birth (used on forms).
N/A	Age of Children N/A	This is *not applicable* to me: I do not need to give an answer (used on forms).
cc	To: Peter Roberts *Cc*: Miguel Fernandez	A copy has also been sent to this person (used in letters and email).
Re:	*Re*: Your email of 27 March	With reference to something (used in letters and email).
Tel.	*Tel.* +44 (0) 025 672389	Telephone number (used in letters and email and advertisements).
RSVP	You are invited to our wedding on 25 May. *RSVP*.	Please reply (used in more polite and formal letters and invitations).
pm	1.00 *pm*	Afternoon or evening (used for a specific time).
am	10.00 *am*	Morning (used for a specific time).
eve.	Phone 025 672389 (*eve.*)	Evening (used in notes and short advertisements).
ASAP	Please do this *ASAP*.	*As soon as possible* (used in friendly and informal messages, email and letters).
vgc	Bike for sale. *vgc*.	Very good condition (used in short advertisements to describe quality).
ono	Bike for sale. $40 *ono*.	Or nearest offer (used after the price in a short advertisement).

Abbreviations	Example	Definition / Use

Use a friendly and informal style when you write to people you know well.

Use a more polite and formal style when you write to people who you do not know well.

Greeting → Saying goodbye

Hi / Pete → Bye for now! / Best wishes

– *Dear Mr Johnson → Yours sincerely*
– *Dear Sir or Madam → Yours faithfully*

Thanking someone for something

– *Thanks for…(a thing, e.g. your email)*
– *It was lovely to get your…(thing)*

– *Thank you for …(a thing)*
– *I am grateful for your…(thing)*

Asking someone to do something

Can you …, please?

I would be grateful if you could …

Telling someone to do something

Send 50 brochures to our Korean office.

Please send 50 brochures to our Korean office.

Offering to do something

Can I send you a brochure?

Would you like me to forward a brochure?

Giving news

Guess what? (+ your news)

You will be surprised to hear that …(+ your news)

Accepting an invitation (saying 'yes')

– *I'll be happy to come.*
– *I'd love to come.*

I would be happy/delighted to come.

Declining an invitation (saying 'no')

– *I'm sorry, I can't make it because …(reason)*
– *I'd love to come but I can't because …(reason)*

– *I am afraid/sorry I cannot come because …(reason)*
– *Unfortunately, I cannot come because …(reason)*

Congratulating someone

Well done!

Please accept my congratulations.

Wishing people a good time

Have a lovely time!

I hope you have a good time.

Sympathising

I'm sorry (for you).

I do sympathise.

Anticipating a future meeting or event

– *See you there!*
– *I'm looking forward to it.*

I look forward to seeing you there.

Closing the letter or email

– *Hope to hear from you soon.*
– *Write soon.*

I look forward to hearing from you.

Audioscript

These recordings are mostly in standard British English. Where a speaker has a different accent, it is noted it brackets.

Please note that the recording numbers below match the track numbers on the audio CD.

Unit 1

 2 (receptionist = Australian; Anna Conti = Italian; Jane Boulson = Scottish; Gordon Mcnamara = American; Eduardo Silva = Portuguese)

a
Anna Conti: My name's Anna Conti.
Receptionist: How do you spell that please?
Anna Conti: A-N-N-A C-O-N-T-I

b
Jane Boulson: I'm Jane Boulson.
Receptionist: Can you spell Boulson?
Jane Boulson: B-O-U-L-S-O-N.

c
Gordon McNamara: Hi. The name's Gordon. Gordon McNamara.
That's G-O-R-D-O-N M-C-N-A-M-A-R-A.

d
Receptionist: What's your first name?
Eduardo: It's Eduardo. E-D-U-A-R-D-O.

Unit 2

 3
Postwoman: I've a parcel for you. Can you sign for it, please?

4
Man at post office:
a This one weighs 2.5 kilograms.
b It's 0.42 kilos.
c It's exactly half a kilo.
d This is a heavy one. 3.6 kilograms.

5
Man at post office:
a That's 0.42 kilograms.
b This one's only 0.09 kilos.
c It's 1.4 kilograms.

6 (customer 1 = French; customer 2 = Saudi Arabian; customer 3 = Chinese; customer 4 = Russian)

a **Customer 1:** I paid about five pounds seventy-five.
b **Customer 2:** I suppose its value is about two hundred and fifty dollars.
c **Customer 3:** It cost ninety-nine cents.
d **Customer 4:** It's not worth a lot. About two pounds.

Unit 3

7
Dr Davidson: Yes, you'd better use my home email. It's d-a-v-i-d-s-o-n-j at p-e-a-c-o-c-k dot co dot u-k

8 (customer 3 = Japanese; customer 4 = Australian)
a **Customer 1:** My email address is a pryce at money dot com. That's a-p-r-y-c-e at m-o-n-e-y dot com.
b **Customer 2:** That's j-o-k-e at f-u-n-n-y-g-i-r-l dot co dot u-k.
c **Customer 3:** Sorry, that should be y-o-k-o dot y at h-a-t-s dot co dot u-k.
d **Customer 4:** You can contact me at p-e-t-e-r-p-i-p-e-r at p-e-p-p-e-r dot com dot a-u.

Unit 5

9
Receptionist: This is a message for Helen Jackson. It's the Leisure Centre here. We're sorry that it's short notice but we've had to change your lesson. Can you come at 5.30 today? In future, your lesson will always be from 5.30 to 6.00 on Monday. If there's a problem with that, give me a ring on 246738. Thank you.

Unit 10

11 (teacher = South African)

Monique's teacher: Next Monday you'll have a progress test to check you're in the correct class. It'll take the whole of the first lesson. Oh, and I nearly forgot, I won't be here so Helen will be running the test. Please come straight up to room 1, as normal. You'll need to be here at 9.00. Make sure you're not late. Helen won't give you any extra time, if you are! The test'll finish at coffee break, about 10.30.

It's a bit like the test you took when you first got here. It's got forty multiple choice questions where you choose a, b, c or d. Then you'll have to write a letter or email. But remember no dictionaries or electronic translators! There are no speaking and listening parts: Helen and I have already decided on your speaking and listening levels. Anyway, I hope it goes well for all of you. Has anybody got any questions?

12 (teacher = South African)

Teacher: Right … your homework for Friday. I would like you to write an essay on a famous person from your country. It can be anyone. The title is 'My hero …' The person doesn't have to be famous outside your country but they must be important to you. I'd like you to write an essay in two parts. The first part should explain who the person is and the second should explain why they are important to you. Okay?

Please use the computers in the study centre to help you. If the person is famous, you might want to look them up. I suggest a book like *Who's Who* or wikipedia. That's w-w-w-dot-w-i-k-i-p-e-d-i-a-dot-o-r-g. But remember I don't want you just to copy out the web page. I want your own words! Is that okay with everyone?

13 (teacher = South African)

Teacher: Okay. On Saturday Barnie's organising a trip up Table Mountain in the cable car. Those of you who are going will have great views up there and you'll also find some beautiful plants and flowers. I'd like you all to do some research for tomorrow's lesson. I want you to find out about one plant you might see on the Mountain. I want you to bring in a picture and describe it to the class. Think of the colour of its flower, how tall it is and where it grows. You can get information on the net. Try www.plantzafrica.com. w-w-w-dot-p-l-a-n-t-z-a-f-r-i-c-a-dot-com. Or go to the Study Centre and find the book *Wild Flowers of the Table Mountain National Park*. Okay, it won't take you very long but I want some good descriptions.

Unit 13

14

Caller: Hello, my name's Ravi Annaji and I'm phoning on behalf of BL Insurance. I won't take two minutes of your time. Do you mind me asking, do you have any health insurance at the moment? People never think they'll get sick or have an accident. Then they need private hospital treatment quickly but don't have the money to pay for it. You don't want that to happen to you, do you? Well, our new Health Insurance plan can save you all the worry. You pay us some money every month and if you do need to go to hospital, we'll pay for it. Simple! Now, perhaps I could fix an appointment to see you. Then I could explain it all to you …

15

Ravi's Boss: You can start selling our new car insurance on Monday. It's a great offer! Only 50 per cent of our normal price. Tell all your customers how cheap it is! Remember, that's half price. On Wednesday I want all the sales people to email me. I want you to tell me exactly how many car insurance policies you've sold. Remember, the special price finishes at 5.00 pm on Thursday. On Friday I want you to all come to a sales meeting at Head Office at 9.00. Okay. Let's get selling …

Unit 14

16 (Kenzo = Japanese)

Kenzo: You have reached the voicemail of Kenzo Asaki. I'm afraid that I'm out of the office until the third of May. Please leave a message. For urgent queries, contact Shona Stevens on 01438 325835. Thank you for calling.

🔊 17 (customer = American)

Shona: Hello. Soloto plc. Shona Stevens speaking.

Customer: Oh, hello. Yes. I was trying to contact Mr Asaki.

Shona: I'm afraid he's out of the office until tomorrow. Can I take a message?

Customer: Oh, could you? It's Mrs Rosen from IWS Ltd. We've recently set up an arrangement with Mr Asaki. I need to know if I order more, can you offer a bigger discount?

Shona: I am afraid you'd have to talk to Mr Asaki about that. I'll get him to ring you back tomorrow, if that's okay? What's your phone number please?

Customer: My direct line's 0206 788 9876.

Shona: That's 0206 788 9876?

Customer: Yes that's right. There's no rush but I'd like to get it sorted this week. I'll wait to hear from him.

Shona: Thank you for phoning, Mrs Rosen. I'll make sure he gets the message. Goodbye.

Customer: Goodbye.

🔊 18 (Marta Miranda = Brazilian)

Shona: Hello. Shona Stevens.

Marta Miranda: Hi, Shona. It's Marta here. Is Kenzo about?

Shona: No, he's on holiday. He's back tomorrow though.

Marta Miranda: Okay. Can you let him know I rang. It's about our meeting on Wednesday. If possible I'd like to move it to Friday?

Shona: Do you want him to give you a ring in the morning?

Marta Miranda: No, that's okay. Just let him know I rang. I'll talk to him sometime tomorrow or email him.

Shona: Okey-dokey. Bye.

Marta Miranda: Bye.

Answerkey

Get ready to write

- Xiaoping is at a hotel/guest house. He is reserving a room.
- He probably wants a single room as he is travelling on his own.

1 b 7   c 2   d 4   e 3   f 8   g 9
2 b 2   c 1   d 5   e 4
3 b T   c T
4

	UK	US
b	8/4/10	4/8/10
c	13/7/08	7/13/08
d	30/9/12	9/30/12

Focus on the alphabet

1 and 2 Anna Konti (Correction: Anna Conti); Jane Poulson (Correction: Jane Boulson); Jordon McNamara (Correction: Gordon McNamara); Edwardo Silva (Correction: Eduardo Silva)

5–7 *Your own answers.* (Check in *Did you know?* to make sure that you have put the month and day in the correct place in the date.)

Class bonus

1, 2 and 3 Student A writes: Mahmoud Boutaleb. 51 Gezira El Wosta Street, Apartment 6, Zamalek, Cairo 1511 Egypt.

1, 2 and 3 Student B writes: George Barras. 84 Chalmers Road, Cambridge CB8 5LL, UK.

Focus on capital letters

1 Last week, I stayed in your New York hotel from Monday to Wednesday.
2 b F   c T   d T
3 The room was cold.
4 Last week, I stayed in your New York hotel from Monday to Wednesday. The room was cold and the shower didn't work. My English is good but the receptionist was rude. She said she didn't understand. Her name is Suzanne Elliot.

8 *Your own answers. Possible answer:*

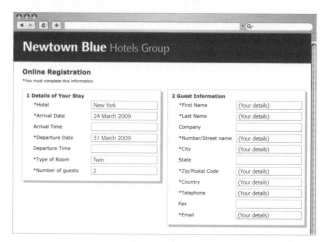

9

Get ready to write

- A postwoman and a customer.
- The customer is signing for a parcel. Her signature is proof that she received the parcel.

1 a Celine Dupont; Don't know
   b Celine Dupont; Mr A Acevedo
2 b 0.09 kg   c £15.00
3 house number / road / city / post code
4 467 Queensferry Road, Edinburgh EH9 7ND

Learning tip

You should not complete the box marked 'For commercial items only'

Focus on weight

1 b Correct   c 0.5 kg.   d 3.6 kg.
2 *Your own answers.*
3 a 0.42 kg   b 0.09 kg   c 1.4 kg

Focus on money

1 b £5,000 c £2.50 d $30.00 e £350.00
2 b $250.00 c 99c d £2.00

5 b T c F (You can tick as many boxes as you want to)
6 a i ii b Send by plane.
7

	Gift\Cadeau		Commercial sample\Enchantillon commercial
✓	Documents		Other\Autre *Tick one or more boxes*

8 international signed for: you probably want to be sure the papers have arrived
9 b Villa 14, The Palm, Al Awir Road, Dubai, UAE
   c a t-shirt
   d 0.42 kg
   e £20.00
10

Unit3

Get ready to write

Personal information	Contact information	Employment information	Financial information
b	a	c	d

1 b 4 c 6 d 7
2 a 9 b 12 c 13 and 14 d 16 e 17
3 a 23 b 25 c 27
4 a 29 b 30 c 33
5 b single woman c married woman
   d single or married woman
6 b Turkish c Chinese d Japanese e Russian
   f Mexican g *Your own answer.*
7

8 *Your own answers.*

1 davidsonj@peacock.co.uk
2 b okej@funnygirl.co.uk   c yoko@dottyhats.co.uk
     d petapiper@pepper.com.au
3 b joke@funnygirl.co.uk   c yoko.y@hats.co.uk
     d peterpiper@pepper.com.au

Unit4

Get ready to write

○ b Where does she come from?
   c What does she do? / What is she studying?
○ *Your own answer.* She might ask: How old is she?

1 b 3 c 4 d 1 e 5
2 Yes

Did you know …?

1 a Mr/Ms/Miss/Mrs + surname
   b Mr/Ms/Miss/Mrs + initial + surname
   c Mr/Ms/Miss/Mrs + first name + surname
2 a Dear Aiko /(Dear Ms Watanabe)
      (Best regards)/ Best wishes / Love
   b Dear Aiko / Best wishes or Love
   c Dear Ms Watanabe / Best regards

3 a My name is Carrie.
     b I come from Glengowrie.
     c I'm studying nursing.
4 *Your own answers.*
5 *Your own answers.*
6 a I like to (verb + expression).
     b I enjoy (verb*ing* + expression).

Focus on sentences

1 b 2 c 4 d 3
2 b finishes   c begins
3 It is very difficult to understand. There are no full stops to help the reader understand where ideas start and finish.
4 I really like sport and listening to music. I love karate. I also enjoy going swimming at the leisure centre. It's very near my house.
5 *Your own answer.*

7 a Dear Mr Reimers
     b Best regards

8 a Japan. Aiko's age depends on when you are writing (the year when you are writing minus 1987).
     b *Your own answer. Possible answer*:
        At the weekend I like to listen to techno music, go for nature walks or paint.
     c *Your own answer. Possible answer*:
        I am an only child and my parents live in Tokyo.
9 *Your own answer. Possible answer*:

From:	**Aiko Watanabe**
Date:	**12 August 2010**
To:	**Lukas Reimers**
Subject:	**My visit to Berlin**

Dear Mr Reimers,

Thank you for being my 'host' in Berlin. I'm really looking forward to staying with you!

My name is Aiko and I'm twenty-three years old. I come from Japan and I'm studying Business at Tokyo University.

At the weekend I like to listen to techno music, go for nature walks or paint.

I am an only child and my parents live in Tokyo.

I am very excited about visiting Berlin because I love to travel and experience new things. I think it's going to be great!

Best Regards

Aiko Watanabe

Unit5

Get ready to write

○ b Denise/Mum   c Robbie   d Helen   e Jet
   f Bubbles

A

1 b By: Malcolm. To: Robbie.
     c By: Malcolm. To: Denise (probably: he writes M not Dad)
     d By: Robbie. To: Helen.
     e By: Robbie. To: Denise.
2 a T Malcolm writes his initial: M. It's short and easy for a quick note.
     b F
     c T
3 b I've gone to the town centre.   c I'll be back at 6.00
     d I'm at the pool.
4 b 1 c 4 d 5 e 3
5 b Malcolm or Denise   c Malcolm and Denise
     d Malcolm and Denise
6 b Can you …?
     c Gone to/At … want to …?
     d Gone to …/Back after …
7 *Your own answer(s). Possible answers*:
     b Malcolm. My light broke. Can you fix it? Thanks. (*Your name*).
     c Malcolm and Denise. Gone to the pizzeria in town. Want to join me at 1.00 for lunch? (*Your name*).
     d Malcolm and Denise. Gone to the cinema. Back after 11.00. (*Your name*).

B

1 b Basketball c the Leisure Centre d 4.00–6.00
2 a ~~Malcolm~~, football ~~practice~~ Leisure Centre ~~Between~~
   11.00 ~~and~~ 1.00

3 a 4.30–5.00
   b 5.30–6.00
4 a Helen b the Leisure Centre c Saturday 13, 3.00–5.00
5 a Malcolm b Tuesday, 2 March at 5.30
6 *Your own answer(s). Possible answers:*

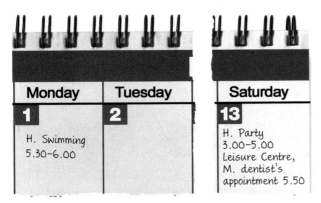

(There is no need to say where the dentist is. The family
already know that!)

Unit 6

Get ready to write

○ b 4 c 3 d 1
○ *Your own answers.*

A

1 b ☹ c ☺ d ☹
2 b Good luck c Wishing you d Best wishes
   e (I) Hope you f Wishing you g Good luck
3 *Your own answer. Possible answer:*
   Congratulations on your Wedding.

4 *Your own answer. Possible answer:*
   To a special couple,
   Congratulations on your Wedding.
   Best wishes
   (Your name)

Focus on fixed expressions

b Congratulations *on your new baby.*
c *Sorry I forgot your birthday.*

Extra Practice

Your own answer. Possible answer:
(Your friend's name.)
Good luck in your new job.
(Your name.)

B

1 a Stefano's grandmother
   b He was very happy.
2 b T
   c F (It is a little more polite and formal than *Hi*. He is
   showing respect!) See Appendix 7.
3 c a d e b
4

Food	Clothes	Books / DVDs
a b c f g i j	b c d e g h i j	d e f g i j

5

I	C	O	L	O	U	R	F	U	L	E
N	G	O	R	G	E	O	U	S	O	N
T	L	U	F	R	S	U	N	D	V	J
E	T	R	E	N	D	Y	G	H	E	O
R	T	A	S	T	Y	T	L	Y	L	Y
E	T	A	E	R	G	V	P	B	Y	A
S	B	J	P	S	U	G	M	W	X	B
T	D	N	V	V	Z	W	E	D	Z	L
I	P	E	G	R	E	A	T	O	R	E
N	L	K	Q	N	O	N	R	W	Q	Z
G	W	T	Q	Y	U	S	E	F	U	L

6 b Now c In the future
7 *Your own answer, e.g.* a chocolates
8 *Your own answer. Possible answer:*
   tasty
9 *Your own answer, e.g.* in the past
10 *Your own answer, e.g.* I ate them last night.

11 *Your own answer. Possible answer:*

[Today's date]

Dear Alexia

Thank you for my birthday present. I love chocolates and these were very tasty. I ate them all in one go last night! Thanks very much.

I'll be in touch again soon.

Love
[Your name]

Unit7

Get ready to write

○ *Your own answers.*
○ *Your own answers.*

A

1 a Stef   b A birthday meal   c At La Trattoria Italian restaurant.   d Saturday 20th March at 8.00pm.
2 a
3 Please let me know ASAP if fyou can come!
4 b At her house   c 28 July, 7.00pm
   d directions to her house
6 *to be* + ing
7 a I'm having a party.   b We're eating at 7.00.
8 *Your own answer. Possible answer:*

Hi!

I'm having a party and I'm inviting all my best friends. I'd love it if you could join us at my new house at 7.00 on 28th July.

There's no parking on Bridge Road, so park in the car park. Come out of the car park and turn right. Go past the first turning and go straight for about 150m. Bridge Road is near the swimming pool. My house is on the left, next to the park.

Please let me know ASAP if you can come!

Love
Isobel

Focus on directions

1 No. Isobel needs to give more detailed information. She needs to think about what information her friends need.
2 a Right.   b a turning/side-road *or* some houses and the swimming pool   c About 150m.   d The swimming pool   e The park.
3 a right   b side-road   c 150   d near   e next

B

1 a The wedding.
2 The reason that she cannot come.
3 b I'll be very happy   c Unfortunately
   d I'm really looking forward to it.   e Thanks

Focus on explaining why you cannot do something

1 b I'm afraid I can't come because I'm visiting my parents on that day.
   c I'm sorry I can't come because I'm studying for exams.
   d Unfortunately, I can't because I'm going on holiday.

4 a *Your own answer. Possible answer:*
      Thank you for your invitation.
   b *Your own answer. Possible answer:*
      Unfortunately, I can't make it because I'm away on holiday with my family
6 *Your own answer. Possible answer:*

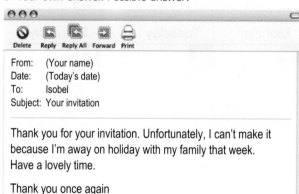

From: (Your name)
Date: (Today's date)
To: Isobel
Subject: Your invitation

Thank you for your invitation. Unfortunately, I can't make it because I'm away on holiday with my family that week. Have a lovely time.

Thank you once again
Love
(*Your name*)

Unit8

Get ready to write

- 2 d 3 a 4 c 5 b
- *Your own answers.*
- *Your own answers.*

1 d

2 b 4 c 1 d 2

3 a F (it is optional) b T c F (it is optional)
  d F (it is optional)

4

> Lakeview Hotel
> Killarney, ~~County Kerry~~
> ~~Eire~~
> ~~12 August~~
>
> ~~Dear Karen~~
>
> ~~How are you?~~ We are having a great time here in Ireland. ~~There is~~ wonderful scenery ~~all round here~~ and ~~the~~ people ~~are~~ very friendly! The weather's not too good but we've got ~~our~~ umbrellas!
> ~~Our journey took a long time. we drove down to Wales and caught a ferry to Rosslaire. On the ferry we met a woman called Mary who told us about lots of places to visit.~~
> Yesterday, ~~we~~ went to the Puck Fair in Killorglin. It's a traditional festival and horse market. They crown a goat and make it king for three days. ~~Then they have a big party. What's great is that it isn't put on for the tourists, the people have been doing it for years and years.~~ There is lots of traditional music! It's amazing!
> Tomorrow we're going to drive round the Ring of Kerry. See you soon.
>
> Lots of love
> Sue and Pete

Focus on giving your opinion

1 a + b – c – d + e + f + g –
2 b ✓ c ✗ (correction: really fantastic) d ✓
3 *Your own answers.* BUT c really awful/really fantastic
4 *Your own answers.*

5 b The museum wasn't too interesting.
  c The food wasn't too good.

6

> ## Old Cataract Hotel
> ### Aswan, Egypt
>
> ~~25 January~~
>
> ~~Dear Carly,~~
>
> ~~I hope you're okay.~~ We're in Aswan ~~at the moment and are~~ having an ~~good~~ excellent holiday. It's a bit hot but the hotel is ~~okay~~ good. ~~It's about a hundred years old and there are~~ views over the Nile with the desert in the background. ~~Lots of little white sailing boats called feluccas go from one side of the river to the other, stopping at the islands.~~ This morning we caught a felucca ~~from the hotel steps~~ to Kitchener's Island. ~~It's a big Botanical Garden with trees with long spikes on their trunks! We walked across the Island and got back on the felucca at other end.~~ At Elephantine Island we saw the Nilometer (the thing the ancient Egyptians used to see how high the water was). We also visited the museum which was ~~boring~~ not too interesting ~~but had a few mummies in the basement.~~ In the afternoon we went to the bazaar. It's really exotic and has lots of little shops selling spices, game boards and rugs. ~~I didn't buy anything but it was very good for window shopping! I think I'll go back another day.~~ Tomorrow we're going on an excursion to see the massive temples at Abu Simbel. ~~The coach leaves at 4.00 in the morning! I hope I get up on time.~~
>
> ~~We'll talk to you when we get back.~~
>
> Lots of love
> Mary (and Adam)

7 *Your own answer. Possible answer*:
In Aswan having an excellent holiday. It's a bit hot but the hotel is good. Views over the Nile with the desert in the background. This morning we caught a felucca to Kitchener's Island. At Elephantine Island we saw the Nilometer (the thing the ancient Egyptians used to see how high the water was). Also visited the museum which was not too interesting. In the afternoon we went to the Bazaar. It's really exotic and has lots of little shops selling spices, game boards and rugs. Tomorrow we're going on an excursion to see the massive temples at Abu Simbel.
Mary (and Adam)

Unit 9

Get ready to write

- Luis is in New York.
- He is waiting for a Greyhound bus to take him to another city.
- He probably doesn't live in the US because he has the Spanish flag on his backpack.

1 a His aunt.
   b He's going to study English and then travel to Boston.
   c He wants her to write to him.
2 b <u>Use contractions, e.g. *can't*.</u> / Never use contractions.
   c <u>Use first names only, e.g. Peter.</u> / Use complete names, e.g. Peter Applegarth.
3 C/O (This is short for *care of*).

Focus on paragraphs

1 a While I was in Boston I went to a really good restaurant that had excellent pasta. ⌐Next week I start work again. I'm not looking forward to it!
   b While I was in Boston I went to a really good restaurant that had excellent pasta.
       Next week I start work again. I'm not looking forward to it!
2 *Your own answer.*

Focus on writing addresses on envelopes

1 b T (He uses capital letters for the state code: *MA*)
   c T
2 a Peter Applegarth / 11 St Leonards Place / YORK / YO9 7ET
   b Suzie Edwards / 802 Font Boulevard / San Francisco CA 94132-4036
3 Mr J Bomberg
   153 Mountbatten Avenue
   Ottawa ON K1H 5V6
   CANADA   (The country is written in capital letters.)

4 *Your own answer. Possible answer:*
   What are you doing in class now?
5 b 1 c 3
6 … I'll never forget the wonderful people in my class.⌐After the course, I caught a Greyhound bus up to Boston and stayed with a friend there. We did all the touristy things in Boston and a lot more! The Italian restaurants in the North End are great.⌐Write to me soon with all your news.

7

Soren Hedegaard
C/O Campbell Language School
537 Argyle Rd
Brooklyn NY 11230-1510
USA

8

Av de la Albufera, 161
28038 Madrid
Spain

10 September

Dear Soren,

How are you? What are you doing in class now? Do you still have Mike as the teacher? We had such a great time in New York together. I'll never forget the wonderful people in my class.

After the course, I caught a Greyhound bus up to Boston and stayed with a friend there. We did all the touristy things and a lot more! The Italian restaurants in the North End are great.

Write to me soon with all your news.

All the best

Luis

Review 1

1 b (see Unit 5)
2 d (see Unit 6)
3 a (see Unit 2). You may also want to write a letter.
4 c (see Unit 7). b and d are not correct because notes and postcards don't usually have many details.
5 a (see Unit 9 and Appendix 7)
6 b (see Unit 4 and Appendix 7)
7 a (see Unit 4). If the person already knows your name, it will be d.
8 a (see Unit 6). Your friend probably knows where you live.
9 a (see Unit 3). b will probably be in Personal Details.
   c will probably be in Financial Details.   d will probably be in Employment details.
10 d (see Unit 5)
11 b (see Unit 7)

12 d (see Unit 5). There is not much space on a calendar. What Peter is doing at drama club is not important.

13 b (see Unit 7, Focus on explaining why you cannot do something)

14 c (see Unit 7). You say sorry before giving a reason why you can't come.

15 b (see Unit 9). The first paragraph focuses on the holiday and the second paragraph focuses on Simone's sister.

16 a (see Unit 9). The post town is in capital letters, all lines start at the same place and there is no punctuation.

17 1b 2a 3d 4c (see Unit 9)

18 a (see Unit 1, Exercise 4)

19 b (see Unit 4 and Appendix 7)

20 b (see Unit 4, Focus on sentences)

21 b (see Unit 4, Focus on sentences)

22 a (see Unit 4, Focus on sentences). Be careful. You do not need a comma here.

23 a (see Unit 4, Exercise 6) enjoy + verb*ing*

24 b (see Unit 8). *Excellent* and *awful* are extreme adjectives and you cannot use *very* or *extremely* with them.

25 a (see Unit 7, Exercises 5–7). We use *to be* + verb*ing* for fixed arrangements.

26 d (see Unit 1). Use capital letters for place names.

27 b (see Unit 1). Use capital letters for languages.

28 b (see Unit 1). Use capital letters for days.

29 d (see Unit 1)

30 a twin (see Unit 1) b full time (see Unit 3)
c fantastic (see Unit 8)

31 d (see Unit 1)

32 a (see Unit 6). We use congratulations for something you have achieved not something that happens every year.

33 a (see Unit 8, Learning tip)

34 b (see Unit 2, Learning tip)

35 d (see Unit 3, Learning tip)

36 c (see Unit 7, Learning tip)

Unit 10

Get ready to write

- a Ulrike Orback (Accommodation officer)
  b Barnie Peters (Social organizer)

A

1

When?	9.00–9.30	9.30–10.30	11.00–11.15	12.00–12.15	12.15–12.30
What?	Welcome talk	Test	Break	Talk: *Living in South Africa*	Talk: *What's on*
Who?	Lesley Smith	–	–	Ulrike	Barnie
Where?	Student Lounge	Rm. 1	Cafeteria	Student Lounge	Student Lounge

2 a 12.00–12.15 or in the break (11.00–11.15). (Ulrike is the accommodation officer.)
b 12.15–12.30 or in the break (11.00–11.15). (Barnie is the social organizer.)

3 Rm.

4 You will probably circle her name, the name of her teachers and the room numbers.

5 Vocabulary and Listening and Speaking/English for Business.

6 ~~The~~ history of rock ~~music — Steve Wroe~~
South Africa: ~~its history and future — Lesley Smith~~
~~The environment:~~ Global Warming ~~or global warning? — Solomon Porritt~~

7 b History of rock c South Africa d Global Warming
(The answers to Exercises 6 and 7 are the same. This is because they show two different ways of focussing on what is important: (1) cutting unimportant words; (2) choosing only the important words.)

8 History of rock

Answer key

9

7–11 July	Monday	Tuesday	Wednesday	Thursday	Friday
9.00–10.30	General English Rm. 1 Mel	General English Rm. 1 Mel	General English Rm. 1 Mel	General English Rm. 1 Mel	General English Rm. 1 Mel
11.00–12.30	General English Rm. 1 Helen	General English Rm. 1 Helen	General English Rm. 1 Helen	General English Rm. 1 Helen	General English Rm. 1 Helen
12.30–13.30	Lunch				
13.30–15.00	Vocabulary Rm. 5 Mel	Listening and Speaking Rm. 6 David	Vocabulary Rm. 5 Mel	Listening and Speaking Rm. 6 David	Lecture: History of rock, Student Lounge
15.00–16.30	Individual lesson Rm. 8 Richard	Individual lesson Rm. 8 Richard	Individual lesson Rm. 8 Richard	Individual lesson Rm. 8 Richard	Individual lesson Rm. 8 Richard

B

1 What does the test include? When is the next test? Where will the test be held? Extra information, e.g. Can I use a dictionary?
2 Yes.
3 Monique writes that the test is at 10.00. It is at 9.00.
4 b F (Monique put the things that are the most important to her at the top of the list).   c T
5 You need to know what the homework is (e.g. the title of the essay) and the date or day you need to give it to your teacher.
6 The teacher will probably tell you the best books or websites to get information from.
7 *Your own answer(s). Possible answers*:
What is the homework?
When do I need to give the homework in?
What books or websites will help me with the homework?
8 a–c *Your own answer(s). Possible answers*:
You may decide that other information is more important and put it nearer to the top of the list.

(Homework)
Essay
Friday
Title: My hero
Famous person from my country.
· Who is the person?
· Why they are important to me.
Look at: 1. Who's who
　　　　2. www.wikipedia.org

Extra practice
Your own answer. Possible answer:

(Homework)
Table Mountain
Research
Tomorrow
Describe a plant
– colour
– height
– where?
Look at: 1 www.plantzafrica.com
2 Wild flowers of the Table Mountain National Park

Unit 11

Get ready to write

a Many students buy second-hand bicycles because they are cheaper. Bike (3) is in good condition and cheap.
b In many countries you can find advertisements for second-hand things in local newspapers, shop windows or on notice boards. It is also possible to buy and exchange things through websites such as www.ebay.co.uk and www.freecycle.org.

A

1 b Steve   c Trisha

104

2 b T (Most sentences are complete. Some sentences that are always used in advertisements have been shortened, e.g. ~~It's in~~ *very good condition.* This is because the reader understands what it means and does not need the complete sentence.)

   c T

   d T (Some also put their telephone number but this is not a good idea.)

3 e b c a d (or e c b a d)

4

	Second-hand			New
Poor	okay	good	excellent	
h	g	f	a c d e	b

5 b 1 c 2

6 a

7 b Details: Sony 750W

Condition: *Your own answer* (Probably *very good condition* or *reasonable condition* because it is only a year old.)

Reason for selling: No longer needed because I'm leaving college.

Cost: £100

   c £50 or nearest offer

   d *Your personal details*

   e *Your email address*

8 b I will pay £20.

   c In exchange, I will teach you French.

9 a Car share wanted

   b I want to go to London on 12 October

   c One small bag

   d I am willing to share the cost of petrol.

   e *Your personal details*

   f *Your email address*

10 Example answers

For sale – Microwave oven

Sony 750W. Very good condition. No longer needed because I'm leaving college. It cost £100. I'm selling it for only £50 (or nearest offer). Email (*your name*) at (*your email address*).

Car share wanted

I want to go to London on 12 October and am looking for a car share. I've only got one small bag and will share the cost of petrol. Email (*your name*) at (*your email address*).

B

2 All the answers are correct. The best answer is (a). If people do not read your advertisement, it is not a good advertisement!

3 very good condition, evenings only

6 a Nearly new.

   b No longer needed.

7 b ~~It's in~~ excellent condition.

   c ~~I'm selling it for~~ £30.

9 *Possible answers*

For sale – Microwave oven

Sony 750W. vgc. No longer needed. Cost £100, sell for £50 ono. Email (*your name*) at (*your email address*).

Car share wanted

To London, 12 October. One small bag. Will share the cost of petrol. Email (*your name*) at (*your email address*).

Unit 12

Get ready to write

- Science.
- *Your own answer.*
- *Your own answer.*
- *Your own answer.*
- *Your own answer.*

1 present

2 b Adam Hart Davis c Ebury Press

   d Non-fiction

3 b When does the story happen?

   c Where does the story happen?

   d Who are the most important characters?

   e What happens?

4 I think it is fascinating.

5 *Your own answers. Possible answers*:

   b I like this book because it explains how science can be fun.

   c If you like popular science, you'll like this.

6 b Science c Computing d History

7 a Romance b Sci-fi c Historical novel d Detective

Focus on linking

1 a and b , (a comma) c and d , (a comma)

2 a ✓

  b ✗ (These are two separate ideas and must be linked with *and.*)

3 Good answer: *The Hound of Baskervilles* is a story about a curse and it's a story about a supernatural dog.

Better answer: *The Hound of the Baskervilles* is a story about a curse and a supernatural dog.

4 a It's set on dark, damp Dartmoor.

  b The main characters are Dr Watson, the American Sir Henry Baskerville and his neighbours.

  c Sir Henry takes Watson with him to spooky Baskerville Hall and solves the mystery.

8 *Your own answer. Possible answer*:

It look like it is a book about people trying to save someone from a dog.

9 a Title: The Hound of the Baskervilles
 b Author: Sir Arthur Conan Doyle
 c Fiction/~~Non-fiction~~

10

> *Your own answer. Possible answer:*
> The Hound of the Baskervilles
> by Sir Arthur Conan Doyle
> (Penguin Classics)
> Fiction
> *The Hound of the Baskervilles* is a Sherlock Holmes detective story. It is a story about a curse and a supernatural dog. It's set in London and on dark, damp Dartmoor more than 100 years ago. The main characters are Dr Watson, the American Sir Henry Baskerville and his neighbours. Sir Henry takes Watson with him to Baskerville Hall and Holmes solves the mystery.
>
> This is a good book. I like it because you never know what's going to happen next. If you like crime fiction and mysteries, you'll like this.
> Giulio Siliotti and (*Your name*)

Unit 13

Get ready to write

○ b
○ a T b T
○ *Your own answer(s).*

A

1 b Notes use complete sentences. / <u>Notes use important words only.</u>
 c Notes give all the information you know. / <u>Notes only give important information.</u>
 d <u>Notes are easy to remember.</u> / Notes are difficult to remember.
3 *Your own answer.* 2 will probably be at the top of the list, 4 will probably be at the bottom!
4 a ~~I~~ work ~~very~~ hard. b ~~I~~ sell more ~~insurance than anybody in the company.~~ c ~~I'm very~~ polite ~~and I'm~~ never late. d ~~All my~~ workmates like me.
5 a Cost? b Age? c Hospital?
6 d *Your own answer. Possible answer:*
  How much does it cost?
7 a *Your own answer.*
 b a ~~What~~ colour ~~is it~~? b ~~Is it~~ new? c ~~Does the price include~~ tax?
8 *Your own answer. Possible answer:*
  Cost? New? Colour? Tax?

B

1 b T c T d T e F
2 a
3 Julie Appleton, Ms Partridge, Mr Davids and Mr Polge
4

Mr Polge (Spixworth) ~~wants to make an~~ appointment ~~to talk about~~ health insurance. ~~Phone back!~~	Ms Partridge ~~at Colney~~ ~~phoned about~~ life insurance. ~~Can you make an appointment?~~
~~Visit~~ Julie Appleton ~~at~~ Easton.	Mr Davids (Dilham) rang. ~~Wants to talk to you about~~ house insurance.

5 Monday
 14.00 Mr Davids, Dilham (house)
 15.00 Mr Polge, Spixworth (health)
 16.30 Ms Gonzalez, Norwich High School
 Tuesday
 14.00 Ms Partridge, Colney (life)
 15.00 Miss Appleton, Easton
 16.00 – Meeting boss (more money!)

Focus on spelling days and months

1 b <u>Tue</u>sday c <u>Wednes</u>day d <u>Thurs</u>day
 e <u>Fri</u>day f <u>Satur</u>day g <u>Sun</u>day
2 June
3 b February c March d April
 f June ✓ g July ✓ h August i September ✓
 j October ✓ k November ✓ l December

Extra Practice

Your own answer. Possible answer:
~~You can~~ start selling ~~our new~~ car insurance ~~on~~ Monday. ~~It's a great offer!~~ Only 50 per cent of ~~our~~ normal price. Tell ~~all your~~ customers how cheap ~~it is! Remember, that's~~ half price. ~~On~~ Wednesday ~~I want all the~~ sales people to email me. ~~I want you to~~ tell me exactly how many car insurance policies ~~you've~~ sold. ~~Remember, the~~ special price finishes ~~at~~ 5.00 pm ~~on~~ Thursday. ~~On~~ Friday ~~I want you~~ all to come to ~~a~~ sales meeting ~~at~~ Head Office at 9.00. ~~Okay. Let's get selling …~~

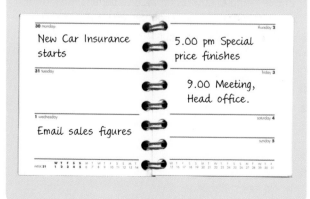

Unit 14

Get ready to write

- Kenzo does not answer the phone because he is out of the office until 3 May.
- a Kenzo is on holiday, at the beach, writing a postcard. He is having a good time.
  b Shona is in an office, working. She is very stressed and overworked.

A

1 a

2 d

3 b 3 c 2

4 b I am away from the office from 19 April until 3 May.
   c I will reply to your message as soon as I can when I come back.

> ### Focus on *from + until / to, for*
>
> 1 b The 2006 Winter Olympics ran from 10 February until 26 February. They ran for 17 days.
>   c The Beatles sang together from 1960 until 1970. They were together for 11 years.
> 2 *Your own answers.*

5 a 23 November (tomorrow)
   b 25 November (He's away for two days: 23 and 24 November.)
   c They should contact Marta Miranda on 01438 325839.

6 *Your own answer. Possible answer:*

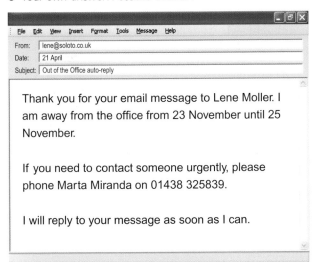

> File Edit View Insert Format Tools Message Help
>
> From: | lene@soloto.co.uk
> Date: | 21 April
> Subject: | Out of the Office auto-reply
>
> Thank you for your email message to Lene Moller. I am away from the office from 23 November until 25 November.
>
> If you need to contact someone urgently, please phone Marta Miranda on 01438 325839.
>
> I will reply to your message as soon as I can.

B

1 Mr Asaki

2 a c b

3 b 1 c 2

> ### Focus on words that people often misspell, mistype or get confused
>
> 1 a Mrs Rosen ordered 500 printer cartridges from the company last week. She wants to <u>by</u> more <u>an</u> says they shouldn't be <u>to</u> expensive. She also wants to talk about other <u>thinks</u> with you. Please phone her back.
>   b Correct spellings: *buy, and, too, things*
> 2 a to b too c two d by e buy f Bye
>   g and h know i our j Who k Their l from

4 a Kenzo
   b Marta
   c a meeting

5

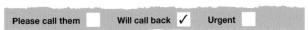

☎ **Telephone Message**

For:	Kenzo Asaki
From:	Marta Miranda
Taken by:	Shona Stevens

7

Please call them		Will call back	✓	Urgent	

8 a Marta Miranda phoned.
   b Can you move the meeting to Friday?
   c No. She said that she'd phone back or email.

9 *Your own answer. Possible answer:*

> **Message**
> Marta Miranda phoned. Can you move the meeting to Friday? She said that she'd phone back or email.

Unit 15

Get ready to write...

- a He has forgotten his password.
  b *Your own answer.*
  c *Your own answer.*

1 c

2 b

3 b *Your own answer.* (You will probably underline all of them but you can tell someone who works for you what to do.)
   c Can you email it to me ASAP, please?

4 b *Your own answer.* (You will probably underline someone who works for you.)

   c Please, be nice to him.

5 b Please telephone Julian Mann.

   c Please get someone to repair the photocopier.

   d Please reply to this email as soon as you get it.

6 *Your own answers. Possible answers*:

   1 your mother or your boss   2 your mother or your boss   3 a workmate   4 someone who works for you   5 a friend

7 *Your own answer(s). Possible answers*:

   b Can you get some cinema tickets for me, please?

   c Can we talk about my pay? Or, even more polite: Could we talk about my pay?

   d Please email the price of the new MP3 players.

   e Please order some more photocopier paper.

Focus on full stops (.) question marks (?) and exclamation marks (!)

1 b ! c ?

2 T

3 a That's wonderful!

   b Thank you for your help.

   c How many have you got?

4 a The facilities at the leisure centre are amazing! There is a swimming pool, a gym and a multi-sports hall! There is also a sauna! Join and enjoy all these facilities free!

   b The facilities at the leisure centre are amazing! There is a swimming pool, a gym and a multi-sports hall. There is also a sauna. Join and enjoy all these facilities free.

---

8 b Computer printer paper   c You want her to send you some paper   d Sandy   e As soon as possible

9 *Your own answer. Possible answer*:

```
●●●                                      ▭
To: Sandy Sharp
From: Your name
Subject: Computer printer paper

We don't have any paper. Can you please send some
ASAP?

Thanks.

Your name
```

Unit16

Get ready to write

  a Rain is coming through the roof in the accounts department.

  b Xiao-Hong wants her to contact Clive Allen at Surebuild to fix it.

  c Xiao-Hong knows her well. She tells her to do something. She writes to her in a friendly, informal way.

1 a

2 b

3 b this is urgent   c you will   d Thank you

   e contact me

4 a T b T c F d F e T

5 a i b ii c iii

6 It is a statement (not a question) and ends with a full stop.

7 Can you send me some envelopes?

8 Could you tell me what you think about the company's new product?

9 I would be grateful if you could arrange a meeting.

10 b 3 c 5 d 7 e 2 f 4 g 1

11 Li wants her to email Mr Takemoto and ask for a price.

Focus on I, you, she, he, it, they

1 you = Clive Allen, it = roof

2 Use a pronoun to refer to a *person* or *thing* that you have already mentioned.

3 Earlier this year, Mrs Ghumman forwarded some of your summer brochures to me. In her letter she said she would be happy to send more. They have been very popular with our customers and we have given all of them away. Please could you send an extra 20?

4 a unclear ('She' can refer to Mrs Ghumman or Mrs Patel)

   b –

   c unclear ('It' can refer to the TEXT2100 or the company)

   d –

5 a *Either*: Mrs Ghumman and Ms Patel work for a travel company. Mrs Ghumman is a sales representative.

   Or: Mrs Ghumman and Ms Patel work for a travel company. Mrs Patel is a sales representative.

   b Clear.

   c The TEXT2100 is a new product from our company. The company has many successful products.

   d Clear.

12 Jo has written a friendly and informal email. This is okay for a friend but Mr Takemoto is not a friend! She needs to write a more polite and formal email.

13 *Your own answers. Possible answers*:

```
 ●●●                                                    ◯

      From:  Jo Grant, Paperless Publishing plc
      Date:  27 May 2010, 10.47
        To:  Mr K Takemoto, Takemoto Industries
   Subject:  Text2100
   ──────────────────────────────────────────────

   Dear Mr Takemoto

   I would be grateful if you could let me know your best
   price for 5,000 units of the Text2100. We would like to
   give it as a free gift to our best customers.

   Thank you for your help.

   Best regards

   Jo Grant
   Paperless Publishing plc
```

Review – Work and study

1 b (see Unit 14) An email (not letter) is also possible if the workmate works in a different office.

2 b (see Unit 16 and Appendix 7)

3 a (see Units 15, 16 and Appendix 7)

4 d (see Unit 10)

5 a (see Unit 12) The other information is useful but not the most important.

6 c (see Unit 11)

7 d (see Unit 14)

8 c (Unit 14) The fact that he was on holiday is not important. He has already said he was out of the office.

9 c (see Unit 16). The reader is confused about who is the native Australian. It could be Thomas Keneally or Jimmie Blacksmith.

10 c (see Unit 13). The price is most important for the boss.

11 b (see Unit 12)

12 c (see Unit 16 and Appendix 7). This is an email to an unknown reader. The style is likely to be more polite and formal.

13 c (see Units 15 and 16). All the other answers are friendly and informal.

14 c (see Unit 16)

15 d (see Unit 16)

16 a (see Unit 15). Question: *Can you help us, please?* Statement: *Please send someone immediately.*

17 a (see Unit 15)

18 b (see Unit 15) a, c and d are not questions

19 b (see Unit 16) books = *They are*

20 d (see Unit 14) *for one hour / until one o'clock*

21 b (see Unit 11) very good condition

22 a (see Unit 11)

23 b (see Unit 13) February

24 a (see Unit 13) Monday

25 c (see Unit 14). Corrected answers: a I want to buy a French grammar book. b The chairs were expensive to buy. d See c.